"Something special happens when a person says, 'I'm willing to be your really good temporary if it helps you find your even better forever.' This is foster care, and it's the compelling message you'll feel resonating from every page of *Missional Fostering*."

JASON JOHNSON, National Director of Church Ministry Initiatives,
The Christian Alliance for Orphans
Author, *ReFraming Foster Care*

"What greater gift can a family offer than to be the hands, words, and love of Christ to vulnerable children in their time of greatest need? It takes the heart of a servant to step into the spiritual, emotional, and relational void that children in foster care have experienced due to chronic and severe abuse. *Missional Fostering* provides invaluable insight to Christ followers, demonstrating how we can help bring hurting children the hope and healing they need to thrive in the years ahead. Thank you, Jon and Dawn, for practicing what you preach and for encouraging others to serve children in such a personal and impactful way."

SAM BEALS, Chief Executive Officer, Samaritas, Michigan

"God is calling His people to action. He is calling us to meet the most vulnerable at their place of greatest need. Through *Missional Fostering*, Jon and Dawn show us the tremendous impact that can be made when people of faith understand this reality, answer God's call, and step into opportunities to reflect God's grace to a watching world. Through the use of humor, emotional stories, and biblical perspective, Jon shares how God has used him and his family to bring gospel hope to many young people in seasons of distress. Oh, that many others would step up and allow God to use them to do the same!"

CHRIS JOHNSON, National Director of Church Partnerships,
Lifeline Children's Services, Birmingham, Alabama

"Jon and Dawn Stone's perspective on love and sacrifice are crucial when tackling the complexities of the child welfare system. *Missional Fostering* challenges readers to confront an uncomfortable question. As we read, we are forced to ask ourselves, 'Should I take responsibility to help youth without families?' As a couple who have grown up in foster care and have learned to thrive because of people like the Stones, we strongly support the message of this book for each of our hearts."

JUSTIN AND ALEXIS BLACK, authors of *Redefining Normal,* re-definingnormal.com

"The Christian church in America has an opportunity in front of her. This new possibility presents itself in a way that is certainly inconspicuous but obviously needed. *Missional Fostering* is a chance to save the world, one child at a time, by representing the love and compassion of Jesus Christ to the most innocent and vulnerable. Jon and Dawn masterfully lay out their case to the Christian community, encouraging the family of God to open our arms and welcome "the least of these" into our homes and our hearts. I highly recommend this book."

JOSH TEIS, Senior Pastor, Southern Hills Church, Las Vegas, and Cofounder of Idea Network

"In a world melting down over politics, social justice, and personal rights, Jon and Dawn Stone and their family provide a refreshing example and difference-making voice! If you are a believer seeking to be a part of the solution, Jon gives a clear path into a powerful and transformational opportunity. I dare you to read this book and to begin giving your life on mission with Him, one life at a time."

CARY SCHMIDT, Senior Pastor, Emmanuel Baptist Church, Newington, Connecticut

JON & DAWN STONE

MISSIONAL FOSTERING

A TEMPORARY ASSIGNMENT

A TREMENDOUS CAUSE

A TIMELESS IMPACT

credo
house publishers

Missional Fostering

Published in the United States of America by Credo House Publishers,
a division of Credo Communications LLC, Grand Rapids, Michigan
credohousepublishers.com

ISBN: 978-1-62586-204-4

Cover and interior design by Sharon VanLoozenoord
Editing by Mike Vander Klipp

Printed in the United States of America
First edition

Contents

INTRODUCTION

An Explanation of "Missional Fostering"

It happens every Christmas season all over the country, all over the world. Businesses put large signs in their windows and on their doors with words to this effect: "Now hiring seasonal employees."

We all know what that means, right? If you get that job, you won't be obligated forever. It is just a short-term gig to help out through a busy season of life. No one applies for that kind of a job thinking that they are going to be employed or obligated forever; that's not what seasonal employees do. Wait for it . . .

That's the idea behind this book. That is the big picture of missional fostering.

Seasonal parenting. Temporary help, as a parent, during a critical time in a child's life. Fostering as a service. Fostering on purpose. Fostering as a calling, a "special ops mission" of sorts with the objective of giving children a place to call home for a short period of their life.

Missional foster parents know that they are just standing in the gap, holding down the fort so that the biological parents can heal and get some much-needed help. Missional fostering can be short term or long term, but the idea is that "We are getting into this space because there are kids who need our help." Missional fostering is about the kids, the cause, and what is it that they need first and foremost.

"But Jon," you might say, "'missional' is not a word."

Yeah, about that, I am waiting for Mr. Webster to read my book and realize that word is worthy of being included in his dictionary. If you have been around church culture for any amount of time, it is a word in our "Christianeze" dialect. I did not invent the word, but it is the perfect word for the trajectory of this work for sure. I call it "missional" because it speaks to me of a specific aim. It is fostering on purpose with purpose. Fostering as a means of gospel therapy for some hurting souls. Missional resonates in the faith-based community because at its root it is a mission.

Think about it this way. There are two lanes in the "fostering freeway." The most commonly traveled lane is the "foster to adopt" lane. The idea of parenting children that are not biologically yours so that you can include them into your family one day is missional. In fact, that is the gospel in a nutshell. A loving father (and mother) rescue innocent and helpless children and adopt them into their family—that is a beautiful snapshot of what the gospel is. To all of you who are in this lane, cheers to you! Fostering to adopt is the best of the best scenarios for fatherless children because families are able to provide a forever home for some who otherwise would not have it. Home run! Grand slam!

I have nothing but the utmost respect, praise, and admiration for those folks. Their impact on a child's life cannot be overemphasized in this lifetime. Hats off to you! Keep up the good work, kids! Most, if not all, of the books on fostering are written for that lane of the fostering freeway. If that is you, or if that is the lane of fostering you will navigate—well done my brotha.

But, fostering to adopt is not the only lane on the "fostering freeway." There is another lane, and it is a lane less traveled. It is not crowded; in fact, the lane that I will call "missional fostering" is wide open: few cars ahead and not many behind either.

Missional fostering is parenting someone else's child for them, in their place, but not necessarily because you are trying to add that child into your family. Missional foster parents may adopt, but their primary motivation is search and rescue. Missional fostering is like triage. A child comes in bruised, battered, and maybe bleeding, but some soul-care physicians step in and help to stop the bleeding while a more permanent room is arranged for the child. Every ER-trained medical professional resonates with the job description I have just described.

Missional foster care parents understand that their role is not to keep the child in the triage unit, but they also know that the triage unit is a necessary stop on the pathway to healing and recovery. Missional parents are able to have their hearts crushed and their feelings trampled by schizophrenic biological parents who can't decide if they really want to get their act together. Missional foster parents are able to see that they are going to be used and sometimes underappreciated, or maybe even taken advantage of. Yet they say to each other, "the kids need us, so we'll get back up, dust ourselves off, and get back into the game." And missional parents may rinse and repeat that cycle over and over again.

Missional foster parents can adopt; in fact, my wife Dawn and I are open to it.

Missional foster parents can be short-term or long-term foster parents; we will briefly explain both in this book. Being missional in your fostering has nothing to do with the duration of time that children are in your home; it has everything to do with the focus of your call into fostering. My wife and I are in the fray because we believe in the cause, the mission; and we believe that God has asked us to help parent these children for a few months of their lifetime. We recognize that we can't adopt every child, and if we did our quiver would be full (not to mention the bedrooms in our home!).

Missional foster care means we get 'em, love on 'em, feed 'em, hold 'em, stabilize 'em, cuddle with the young ones, high-five the big ones, and then watch 'em drive away to a long-term home so that they can begin their reunification plan or their foster-to-adopt plan.

Mission accomplished.

Finding Your Own Lane

Have you ever thought of taking a job like that? What do you have that God could use to help the cause? The fact that you have spent some of your own bread on this book indicates that you probably have a good heart and some sort of an interest in the topic. Do you have an extra bedroom in your home, an extra seat in your car? Do you live in an empty nest and wonder or wish that you could have some of the joy and laughter of children back in your home again, but you don't want the long-term commitment? That's where missional fostering comes in.

I am hoping you will see that there is a lane that is wide open to you. Missional foster parents are temporary, stopgap, stand-in, interim caregivers for a short period in the life of a child. Missional fostering may not result in long-term relationships with a child, but it may result in the child having a renewed relationship with their parents or some other foster parents who are looking to adopt. Mission accomplished because the goal of the mission was not populating your family, it was stabilizing a needy child!

Does it really take Kirk Cameron to make a movie about fostering in order for the faith-based community to get involved? (I love Kirk Cameron, and I hope he does make a movie about it by the way). Missional fostering is an action that is driven by the command from Jesus to love our neighbors as ourselves! Fatherless children are our neighbors, movie or no movie. (Note to self: mention something to Kirk.)

My goal is to recruit foster-care parents by making you aware of the need. My approach in this book will be to dialogue about the process so that you can walk inside our home and see what fostering with a missional mindset is like. By the time we land the plane, I hope that you will see how you can declare the love of God to some children who may never have heard about our "Good, Good Father." (Sounds like a great name for a song!)

Missional foster care parents are not trying to PREACH the gospel to the fatherless and orphans. Missional foster care parents DISPLAY it. Missional foster parents often hail from the faith-based community. Missional foster parents still believe that Jesus had it right when he said, "Let your light so shine before men, that they may see your good works and glorify your Father in heaven" (Matthew 5:16).

Missional foster parents are able to do triage in their homes. Missional foster parents don't need a lot of high-tech equipment, nor do they need to spend years of their life in fostering schools. Missional parents recognize that their call is to be parents for their own children and for some other people's children. I'm not saying that parenting has ever been easy, but think about this: you spent the first 18 years of your life being trained by a parent. Then you took a few years off to find a mate, and then you began the parenting process yourself.

Parenting is something many of you are already doing right now! You are already cooking meals, driving kids all over creation like a glorified Uber, and tucking a couple of precious jewels into bed at night! What is one more? Most of you already have the rooms you need in your home. Many of you even have bunk beds already for Pete's sake! And if you've never yet had a family of your own, I'm guessing that since you're reading this book, God has already planted a thought, a seed in the soil of your mind.

Would You Do It?

Let's go into a hypothetical at this point. Suppose my wife and I are driving down the road on an interstate near your home. And, just for effect, suppose we still had our 3 bio children in our home, so that our little SUV was complete with 5 bodies: 2 adults and 3 children. We are driving to your home to stay with your family the Saturday night before we share about Missional Fostering in your church on Sunday. With me so far?

Then, just for the sake of drama and effect, as we are rolling down the road, listening to K-LOVE, we are almost to the exit to get to your home, and we are involved in a very serious accident. You roll up on the scene of the accident, recognize us and what has happened. Dawn and I are rushed to the hospital, but the three children are fine.

Do you have the picture? You see our three children are standing there on the side of the road. They need someone to care for them for a little bit until mom and dad can get back on their feet. What would you do? Would you volunteer to the officers at the scene to take my kids for a few weeks or so until Dawn and I could get well? (It doesn't work that way, but for the point of the illustration, let's say it was that easy. You just volunteer to the police officer to take our kids.)

Would you be willing to care for our kids like they were your own? Would you give them food, a warm bed and safe place to stay? Would you help them to get to school or to doctor appointments? When my kids cried at night because they missed their mom and dad, would you comfort them? Would you try to divert their attention to other things so they wouldn't dwell on the trauma that has come into their life?

Then, when Dawn and I were better, would you seek to reunite them with us, knowing that they were never really your children, but that you were just being a fill-in? Would you get attached to my kids? Absolutely, because God has given to us amazing children! Would you be sad when they left? Probably a little. Would you be a little attached? Probably, especially if they spent a couple of months with you. Would you be happy that they were able to reunite with us? 100%!

Why would you take my kids in? Well, if you know Dawn and I and if you happen to like us, you would do it out of love for our family. Who wouldn't?

What if you didn't know the driver of the car? What if the driver and his wife were totally unknown to you? Could you do it then? What if the driver of the car had been drunk and was involved in a DUI? What if the driver and his wife were in trouble with the law and they were both spending some time in lockup to sort things out?

Would you be willing to take the kids then? Would you be willing to stand in as temporary parents until the driver and his wife were able to get back on track? To Dawn and I, the answer is a great big fat "YES!" That is what Jesus meant when he said to love our neighbors—it is loving *all* of our neighbors, which just happens to include foster kids.

That is missional fostering in a nutshell.

You in? You interested in hearing more?

The Crisis at the U. S. Southern Border

This book was conceived in the early months of 2021. At the end of the writing of this book, the U. S. government had just transitioned from the Trump administration to the Biden administration.

Over the last two decades, America has seen a sharp increase of children migrating from Central America into the southern states. It is not in the scope of this book to discuss the arguments as to why children began to be dropped off at our southern border, but the fact of the matter is that there are thousands of migrant children left at our southern border every year. While this has been going on for years, it is unquestionably true that the influx of fatherless children has increased in the early parts of 2021. Many of these children have been dropped off by their parents, and some are trafficked by for-hire smugglers who leave the children at the border for a price. These smugglers are often referred to as "coyotes."

At the time of the writing of this book, BBC news "unofficially" estimates that more than 15,500 unaccompanied children are in U.S. custody.[1] In February, 2021, more than 9,500 children who were unaccompanied by their legal guardians were detained by American officials.

What do we do with these children? Please don't lay down your politics card. Please don't tell me that your political persuasion will cause you to look away from destitute children who need a loving mother and father to care for them! The frightened children standing there in the collection facilities don't have any political preferences. Some of them are too young to know even where they are—all they know is that they just don't see mommy or daddy anywhere! They were brought here of no fault of their own. They were led, pushed or thrown across the border. They are now sitting in facilities in our southern states as our government tries to decide what to do next.

The Christian community needs to be prepared to jump into action at the minute our authorities ask for help. This is not an issue of whether you are a Republican or a Democrat or a Libertarian; this has nothing to do with social justice; this is not an issue of whether or not we should have open borders; this is an issue of LOVE. What does

1 BBC.com

God want His people to do? Do these children qualify as orphans or fatherless children? Absolutely they do—that is exactly what they are.

The bigger question is, what will you do? A quick, distracting game of Candy Crush will not make the problem go away! Mission-minded foster parents will rise up and stand in the gap for these fatherless and motherless children.

TWO DISCLAIMERS:
1. No Initials After Our Name

So you should know that neither Dawn nor I are psychologists, doctors, psychiatrists, medical professionals, LPC's, LPCC's, LCSW's, LMFT's, or even just MSW's. In fact, we don't have any initials after our names! Furthermore, we did not go to college to study "Foster Care Education." Nope, none of that, you are reading just plain ol' Jon and Dawn, foster parents at large.

To any professional who has trained, studied, sacrificed, and suffered through the challenges of getting into the area of social work, our hats are off to you. You people work tirelessly in a field where there is little reward for sure. Our daughter is presently a senior in college majoring in sociology. I think part of her life choice is in part due to observing what you do day-in and day-out.

If you are one of those professionals who has initials behind your name on your business card, then we humbly ask you to pardon our insufficient clinical analysis and excuse our "bottom shelf" approach. We are writing from the trenches, not from a professional building. We are still the ones that you see running our fosters around to therapy sessions, playing catch, chasing little ones all over the house and tucking them in bed at night. We hope you will appreciate our passion to make fostering a topic of conversation, particularly in our faith-based community.

Our goal is simple: to recruit adults of all ages into providing foster care for the youths who desperately need a safe place for a little while in their journey. Not everyone will be a foster-to-adopt family. Not everyone will be able to do missional fostering; I totally get that. Some who read this book will be "respite" (babysitters) for foster parents—that will also be a win for the home team.

We have come to call our fostering "missional" because we are not necessarily trying to add another child into our permanent family. That may happen before it is all over, but our mission is to be a safe spot for as many youths as we can as the adults around them try to decide what is best for the child.

This book is not a sermon, nor is it a sermon series that has been edited. It is not a "How-To" manual of foster care. It is not an encyclopedia or a dissertation that I have decided to publish. We are not professionals, so please don't quote us! This book is just a narrative about our journey into what we have come to call "missional foster care." We jumped in the water because we saw kids who were drowning, and we felt like God wanted us to jump in the pool with some floaties to help stabilize some vulnerable yet precious children. I hope you will hear the heart behind this document and see beautiful faces of innocent children who have been handed a pretty tough lot in life. We want them to give voice to their cries!

2. A Word to Our Foster Kids

It is truly presumptuous of us to think that you would ever see this book or pick it up to read. There aren't any pictures, and I have tried to tone down my dad jokes, but if you just happen to be reading, we have so many things we want to say to you.

First, we want to tell you again that we absolutely love you and we enjoyed the time we shared in our home together. We hope you enjoyed the meals, the drives in the Mustang, the hot doughnuts from Krispy Kreme, and of course, the world-famous burgers. Both Dawn and I want you to know that you shaped our hearts, minds, and our understanding of what trauma can do to a child. We had no idea what you had been through, we're just glad to have shared some time with you.

You are a champ! We admire you and we are pulling for you—remember my promise to stand and cheer loudly at your graduation with your name painted on my bare chest! (I can't understand why none of you have agreed to this genuine gesture of unconditional love. The offer remains on the table if you graduate from college.)

We still laugh with fondness at many of your times with us. Our nightly "debriefs" were our best attempts at trying to help put some structure and organization into your life at a time when your life was in the middle of upheaval.

Dawn and I have kept pictures of almost every one of you. There were a couple of you who got out without us snapping a quick photo, but only one or two. Your photos pop up on our social media memories and we have been able to reminisce about the absolute best of times that you shared at our home. We might remember some of the not-so best times as well, but who wants to rehash that? Not me.

There is always the risk that one of you could find this book and realize that one of the stories we are telling is yours. We hope you will hear the love and fondness in our hearts for each of you. You will notice that we have changed your name so that your identity is protected.

We also want you to remember that we didn't get into fostering with the plan of writing a book. We didn't journal every detail, so there is a chance that a detail or two are confused. (Hey, you forgive us, and we will forgive you for what you did too, *wink wink*.)

Most importantly, we also would like to thank you for helping us to see the parts of us that were broken. We are forever indebted to you for helping us to grow in love, grace, and forgiveness.

Your hurt shaped us; your tears challenged us; your cries changed us and made us better people. You were one of God's kindest gifts to us.

To those who came to our home early on in our fostering "career," I say to you, "Whoa Nellie, we are really sorry!! We learned so much more over time." I wish you could drop back in now, without the "magic brownies," of course. We are not perfect foster parents as you well know. Although you may not have realized it, we were learning as you were teaching us lessons.

Lastly, we want you to know that you will always have a place at our table on holidays. We have told you before and we still mean it, you are always welcome on "wing night." We love you all!

Discussion Questions

1. What is your experience with foster care? Who do you know that was in foster care at some point in their childhood? Do you know anyone who was adopted out of the foster system?

2. What are some of the mistaken preconceived ideas people have about foster kids? Did anything you heard in this chapter shed a new light on the idea of fostering?

3. How does "missional foster care" picture the gospel narrative? (How do you see sin, punishment, rescue from the Hero, and the good news?)

4. Jon and Dawn sound like they have come to love the kids that were in their home. Is that what you expected to hear? Please explain your answer.

5. In your own words, what is the difference between missional fostering and fostering to adopt? Of the two, which one is more appealing to you?

CHAPTER 1

Is There a Cause or Not?

There is a great cause that warrants missional fostering.

Thousands of years ago a young teenager stood on a Judean hillside and asked the king of Israel a question. Five words. Not a long question, just a short five-word question: about as many words as the average teen can organize into a complete thought, right? Only five words, but what powerful words they are: "Is there not a cause?" (1 Samuel 17:29). His point was clear. Sure, the giant is real. Yes, he looks like Shaq on stilts. Yes, the task is daunting, and a bit scary, but, King Saul, "Is there not a cause?"

Odds are, you picked up this book or downloaded it to your device because something about the words "missional" or "fostering" resonated with you. In some way you heard a "cause" or a mission or a crisis that prompted an action from you. That is pure gold.

Maybe you know a foster child or a foster parent who lives on your street and you have wondered about what the fostering life was like. Maybe you are a follower of Christ, so you recognize that you are living a missional life already, and something about the idea of making a difference with kids resonated with you. Maybe you are considering foster care, maybe you are already in the ranks;

whatever the case, I am glad you are flying with us today—buckle your seat belts and stay in your seats, because we expect to have some choppy paragraphs ahead in our trip through this chapter. Please know that you will get through this chapter, but some kids you read about might not.

Are you aware that every day in America there are approximately 424,000 children in foster care? That's almost half a million. Pause to process: 424,000! According to UNICEF, there are 153 million orphans in the world, although everyone familiar with the system would know that there are more—many, many more than that.

Almost one hundred forty times every day in California, a child is removed from their home and placed into foster care.[1] Allow that last sentence to hang out there for a minute. Don't move on just yet—140 times a day in California alone. That's 980 times a week, about 4000 times a month, and right at 50,000 times a year . . . IN CALIFORNIA ALONE.

Of the 424,000-plus children in foster care every day in the United States, over 60,000 of them live in California.[2] Statistics show that if a child remains in foster care for more than 24 months, that 44% of them will be placed in three homes, and 15% of them will be placed in up to 5 homes.[3] Is it any wonder that foster youth struggle with feeling loved, accepted and appreciated?

The first question that comes to my mind is "Why?" Why so many?

A Biblical worldview would inform us that this world of almost 7.7 billion people is filled with people who are broken way down in their very core. All the way down in the fabric of our DNA there is a thread of sin that runs deeply through every human that is the result of a choice made by our father, Adam (Romans 5:12). Adam sinned, his sin nature was passed along to every descendent—which happens to include you, by the way. That sin nature has given birth to sin choices that harm us and even hurt those around

1 clccal.org
2 clccal.org
3 clccal.org/resources/foster-care-facts/

us. We are born with an ability and a desire to sin, and for some, the cocktail of choice is self-pleasure, even if it means harming innocent children in the process. With sin came abusive parents, neglected and abandoned children, the child sex trade, and the list goes on. The reason there are so many children in foster care is because there is a pool of 7.7 billion sinners in this world.

Think about this for a moment: child abusers don't take vacations, and they never give their victims time off for good behavior. They do not observe holidays, and they don't reduce their hours on the weekends. They do not have pity on the children they harm; for many, that child is a means to self-pleasure. Abusers are like that old Energizer Bunny: they keep going and going and going.

For some child victims, it's like that old movie *Groundhog Day* where Bill Murray is trapped in a time warp and every day is the same thing over and over again until he is transformed. Many children will keep waking up each morning only to relive their worst day over and over and over again. Some kids feel like they are trapped in a nightmare from which they can never wake.

Some children will be locked in rooms by themselves. They will cry but no matter how long or hard, no one will ever come to help them. They will weep, scream, bang their heads on the floor, and sit in wet diapers for hours. Their stomachs will growl, their lips will quiver from the cold, and they will whimper, yet no one will come through the closed door to check on them. (I am choking back tears as I type right now.) At some point in their young lives they will begin to believe that they must not be very important. Therefore, they must not be very valuable. Those thoughts spiral into a thought process that says, "I can trust no one, I must take matters into my own hands." They will doubt, resist, and refuse to attach to a parent / caregiver because that individual does not take care of their needs.

Some children will be exploited. Ugh. My fingers just can't seem to type out the dark words that describe the heinous acts that are perpetrated on these young victims. These acts are well documented and can be found quickly in any search engine. Go ahead and check, BUT BEWARE. The stories that you read about this abuse are not easily forgotten. Reading about trafficked children is mind-altering. Go there if you want, but I warn you that those are dark and murky waters . . . and know that there are children who are trapped in that prison until help comes.

Some children will be trafficked for financial gain. At large events like the Super Bowl, the heightened demand for sex leads to the trafficking of children as well as women. More than 100,000 children are trafficked for sex every year in the United States.[4]

Reading that makes me feel a little dirty. And angry. And disgusted. I must do something! You must do something! Is that a cause? Of course it is.

Day after day, week after week, month after month and sometimes year after year, children are traumatized and even victimized by people that they know, love, and trust. By an act of God's mercy, some children's Sheol will get noticed—maybe by a teacher who sees some bruising or a neighbor who hears the screaming. The authorities will get notified, the victims will be examined, investigations will be commenced, and the children may be removed from their waking nightmare.

If you advance to the next paragraph or the next chapter hoping the topic will lighten up a bit, know this. Some children's abuse will never be noticed or discovered. They will continue to live as prisoners in their own home.

No one is asking us to conduct investigations, take photos, stakeout shady joints around town or break down the doors to rescue abused children. This is America, people! Our country already has these agencies in place. Good guys are already monitoring the dark web for child sex trafficking language. Undercover agents are already posing as teenagers online, reeling in those predators filled with lust who are trying to meet up with vulnerable children. No one is asking us to do the heavy lifting. Let's leave that up to the trained professionals who wear bulletproof vests and capes and have superpowers!

So, what am I asking you to do? What is our role; your role? What should you be doing; what can you do? The fact that you have not put down the book yet is a very good sign, ya know. I see good things ahead for you, but I will warn you, it could get messy.

---

4 Itsapenalty.org

For many of us, we feel bad for about 10 minutes. Kids being harmed and violated by adults, now that's just not cool. Everything inside of us screams at the top of our voices—RESCUE THOSE CHILDREN FROM THAT MESS!

Then what? What happens when we save the children from their unsafe situation?

Well, most of us thank God to hear that a child has been rescued, and then we will go into the kitchen, open the fridge and divert our attention on to something more pleasant, like those leftovers that would make the perfect late-night snack.

Kids' lives don't improve just because we stop thinking about them. *OUCH!* That hurts, and unfortunately it hits close to home—probably very close to where you are sitting right now.

But know this, the children who need our help simply don't go away or get helped because we stop reading. Rescuing a child is part of the solution for sure, but then what should we do with the child?

The helpless victims get removed from their dungeon of waste, abandonment, and abuse, but where should they be placed? (I don't want you to miss the hook: here it is!)

In foster homes, that's where! In loving, safe, and secure homes where the children can learn to cope with what has just happened and begin the lifelong journey of healing.

What about when there are not enough foster homes to place all of the children? What then? (Hello? "Bueller? Bueller?") What if there aren't enough foster or adoptive homes in a county or a state?

Now we are at pay dirt. We are standing at Ground Zero. The answer is to volunteer to engage in missional fostering: parenting a child who may never be a part of your family by decree of a judge, but will always be a part of your heart in this lifetime and . . . just maybe beyond.

I believe that God wants YOU to do something about it. That's right, you! Mr. White-Collar Professional who is having Siri read this to you as you drive to and from work. Yes ma'am, in your minivan with an empty seat. Yup, empty nesters, you guys have the experience necessary and unlike Bethlehem of years gone by—YOU HAVE ROOM IN THE INN!

My goal in this book is to help you to see the need. The need is great, but the homes are few. Every month when our FFA (foster family association) meets and puts out literature there is always a reminder to organically recruit our friends into the ranks of caregivers so that we can house every child who needs one.

Dawn and I feel that God wants us to add a voice for those whose voices are not heard. To the fatherless, the orphans, and the fosters, we hope this book will be a voice for them. Maybe this will be a voice for our Father to use to cause you to hear the cries for help that scream all around every one of us.

Hopefully by the time we land this plane you will be more informed about this underserved people group in America. Awareness of the great need is for sure the starting point; it was for me.

It has been said that we see what we look for. Sounds about right, so look for injustice in this next paragraph. Look for it, see it, think about it, and let's dialogue about it.

Awareness of the Need

Here are some facts from Alternative Family Services that shed some light on the monumental issues that are present in foster care.

- The average time a youth spends in foster care is 20 months.
- 32% of foster children are younger than 5.
- 28% of foster children are between the ages of 6 and 12.[5]
- 40% of foster children are between the ages of 13 and 21.[6]
- By the time foster youth are 24, only half of them will have a stable and steady employment.
- 50% of all foster youth will develop a substance abuse problem.
- 81% of all of foster males will be arrested in their lifetime.[7]

---

5 Ibid.

6 Ibid.

7 Ibid.

- After the age of 18, one-third of all males and three-fourth of all females who have been in the foster system will rely on government assistance.
- 45% of all foster youth will never graduate from high school.[8]
- 38% of all foster children in California will never find a permanent placement. They will never have a forever home.
- 25% of all foster youth have attempted suicide by the time they are 17.[9]
- The suicide attempt rate for foster youth living in a group home was 2.6 times higher than youth living in a foster home.[10]
- By age 19, 48% of the girls in foster care had been pregnant, and 46% of them had been pregnant twice.[11]
- 60% of child sex trafficking victims have been in the foster care system.[12]
- Foster care students are 5 times more likely to get suspended from school than non-foster students.[13]
- 80% of children in foster care have significant mental health issues.[14]
- 80% of inmates who are incarcerated spent time in the foster system.[15]

What did you see? You see what you look for, what did you see?

Did you see stats? Maybe just some troubling numbers on a page? Did you see problems and inconveniences? Did you just see the words, "Suicide, drugs, alcohol, teen pregnancies, suspensions, prison, inmates, sex trafficking" and think, "hurry up and tell us a feel-good story?" Some of you read those stats and you just saw another drama that you don't have time for.

---

8 fostersuccess.org
9 chosen.care
10 Ibid.
11 providence.org
12 sosillinois.org
13 kidsdata.org
14 ncsl.org
15 fostercare2.org

Some people look at problems only long enough to realize that they need to look away.

However, there were some of you who looked at those stats and you didn't see more bad news. Those of you in this category saw humans with real heartbeats, real lives, and real eternal souls. You saw tiny, small, innocent, helpless, powerless, defenseless faces that are connected to abused bodies.

Some of you heard "mission." You read those words and you thought "ministry." It is those of you who I would like to engage with. You are the ones who hold the keys to the kingdom of God for some young kids who wonder if God is really good at all.

It was Jesus who told a story of a Levite and a priest who did something similar when they saw a need. A couple of religious do-gooders saw a man lying in the middle of the road bleeding out. In one Bible translation it says that this man was left "half dead" (NKJV Luke 10:30). Those religious do-gooders saw the blood, trauma, and hurt, and they turned their heads and walked away as fast as they could (Luke 10:25-37).

Good people skirt the needs of fatherless children because they are not personally impacted. It's not their child, not their grandchild, no relation to them, so they just try not to think about this difficult topic any longer!

Just to finish the story, the priest and the Levite who walked away were not praised by Jesus for their lack of action. In fact, the one who was called "good" was the Samaritan who rolled up his sleeves, got into the middle of the mess, and cared for the injured man.

Go ahead and turn the page or turn the book off if you would like, but doing so won't make the problem go away. Skipping to the next chapter will not stop the hurt and harm. I'm pretty sure that putting our fingers in our ears and closing our eyes to the problem is not the answer either.

Dialogue About Your Role

What should you do?

Great question, so glad you asked. I hope you will engage with us in this dialogue about your role in the solution. Let me put this on the bottom shelf, down where us simple thinkers can grasp it. We want you to pray with us, think with us, talk with us, laugh with us, cry with us, and plan with us to become involved in helping to stabilize some young ones who have not been able to get off on a good foot in their life.

For now, let's just talk; I'm not a salesman and there are no quotas to meet. Let's just talk. And think. And process what is happening to children in our world. What if, in the course of this book, we could show you the joys, hardships, and overwhelming rewards of true religion in its purest form (James 1:27)? If you could walk into our family room, tour our home, listen to our stories and observe the realities of what the role of a mission-minded foster care parent goes through, would that interest you?

And Yes, There Is a Hole in the Wall

At the time of this writing, there is a hole in the drywall. It's the size of a teenaged fist. Over the weekend one of our youth wasn't able to self-regulate. When she settled down about an hour later, she walked down to the kitchen and handed us a one-page apology letter. Read it slowly, it was hand-written on notebook paper, and it was stained with her tears. Here's what she wrote:

> Dear Dawn, I'm sorry for making a hole in your wall. Sorry for all the things I do . . . I am not a good person, I know. I hope God can help me reading the Bible. I am sorry for every trouble I do. I would not mind if you sent me to prison for all of the trouble . . . I am double, triple sorry . . . I understand if you are angry. P.S. Thanks for being there.

(Choking back tears right now.) This is foster care. It is raw and real.

This is what we live for. These moments. That moment when a child knows they have blown it and now we get to teach them about forgiveness, love, and reconciliation. If this were Sunday and you were sitting in a chair in front of me, I would say, "We live to give and show the gospel!" In those precious seconds as we read the apology note, I listened to Dawn preach a gospel message of grace that would have brought a Presbyterian to their feet! Dawn knows grace, and she was dishin' out heapin' scoops of God's love, forgiveness, and grace after she read this letter. Priceless.

We want this to feel more like a story than a lecture. I admire Dawn greatly for what she has shown me about loving people. She is a champ! It is not hard to see why our foster youth love her the most. It also might have something to do with her crazy-good culinary skills, but hey, who is jealous? Not me.

Display the Love of Christ

For those who will finish the trip with us, I think you will agree that in foster care, we are showing the love of God through acts of kindness to youth who have become disillusioned about why God would allow such things to happen to them. WWJD? I think he would get into foster care. Maybe, just maybe you will see that loving these defenseless children of God is something that God is placing on your radar—that's what we are shooting for.

Any Tom, Dick or Harry can love people who are nice to you. Here's what Jesus said a bit over 2000 years ago.

> But if you love those who love you, what credit is that to you? For even sinners love those who love them. And if you do good to those who do good to you, what credit is that to you? For even sinners do the same. And if you lend to those from whom you hope to receive back, what credit is that to you? For even sinners lend to sinners to receive as much back. But love your enemies, do good, and lend, hoping for nothing in return; and your reward will be great, and you will be sons of the Most High. For He is kind to the unthankful and evil. Therefore be merciful, just as your Father also is merciful. Luke 6:32-36

If you tell me you like the book, I will say "I love you." If you buy the book and send it to all of your friends in your connect group, I will really, really love you. I love the people who play nice, don't you?

The test of your love is not whether you can love nice people—anyone can do that! But can you love displaced, disoriented, and destructive youth who may not love you back? According to Jesus, that is the test of your love. Is your love for Christ deep enough to love children that are not biologically related to you? Can you love them as if they are your own? And if and when they put a fist-shaped hole in your wall, can you still love them then?

The thing about fostering, whether you are "missional" or "foster to adopt," is that you've gotta get down in the trenches: the trenches that are knee deep in you-know-what. Yes, you know exactly what I mean and what I am describing but not saying. Why do you have to get in you-know-what? Because that's where the kids are, knee deep in you-know-what. Their life seems like a never-ending pile of you-know-what. The longer they stay in you-know-what the more they believe that they are worth you-know-what!

Do you see the cause? Do you see children? Fatherless children? Orphans? Wards of the state? Kids who are without a place to go for Christmas dinner when they age out of the system? If something were to happen to you and your mate, would you want someone to open their home for your grown children on the holidays so they can experience family on those occasions? Of course you would. Know this, many kids will eat Christmas dinner at Denny's when they are 19 because they never were transplanted into a forever home.

Missional fostering says, "I see the cause and I want to be a part of the solution. I know that there will be holes in our walls and stains on the carpet and I recognize that I'm probably going to get F-bombed along the way if I foster teenagers!" Can you stay on the job long enough to point them to a God who is crazy about them? Maybe you will get the privilege one day to tell them that God wants them in your home so that you can show them what a loving father looks like. That is the cause of fostering.

It is my sincerest hope that this book will awaken the slumbering saints and open the homes of every reader. Maybe you aren't ready to bring someone into your home at this time, but maybe you will see something that you can do—a way you can get involved. The gripping stories of fosters, the mesmerizing homily of a speaker, or even the sadness of the statistics might motivate you to take an action, and I hope that it will. But what gets people started in a cause is usually not what keeps them going. What causes people like you to keep reading this book about fostering is mission.

"Is there not a cause?" (1 Samuel 17:29). Yes, there is a huge cause about which I will tell you more in the next chapter.

But what if you really understood that you could change the trajectory of a child's life forever? You can! Yes you! More on that in the next chapter.

Discussion Questions

1. What is the reason that you bought this book? What were you looking for? What did you expect to hear?

2. Jon spoke of a Biblical world view that would explain the reason that so many children are in foster care in America. What is the role of sin in the process? (Please answer within the framework of Romans 5:12.)

3. Why do you think there is a still great need for foster homes? In your opinion is it a lack of awareness, a lack of interest, or something else?

4. Of all of the statistics that were listed in the section "Awareness of the Need," which one or ones impacted you the most?

5. Explain how foster-care parents (particularly missional ones) display the love of Christ to those in their care. Do you think all foster kids respond in a positive manner? If not, why not?

CHAPTER 2

Pro-Life = Pro-Foster!

Missional foster care is the back-end process of the pro-life movement.

If you say you are pro-life, then I believe you will need to be pro-foster care. I don't see any other options.

At lunch one afternoon, one of our Santa Barbara County supervisors was talking with me about the foster-care system. He made a statement because he knew that I was a pastor, and he knew that our friendship would allow him to be candid. He said, "I know that you guys have to preach against abortion. I just wish that pastors would spend more time talking about what they are *for* and less time talking about the things that they are *against*." Excellent feedback!

I get it. Be against abortion. And be for foster care and community involvement in the lives of these children who didn't get aborted. I am not going to preach against abortion in this chapter, but I will pontificate about another alternative I see to abortion. Just a simple statement I hope you will allow me to defend. If you say you are pro-life then you must be pro-foster. Pro-Life = Pro-Foster.

A Better Option

When Pam finally went to the hospital, she was so sick she could hardly stand. The year was 1987, and Bob and Pam were missionaries in the Philippines. Pam contracted amoebic dysentery, which is usually transmitted through the drinking water. Although this type of ailment is common in other countries, Pam fell into a temporary coma and had to receive some strong antibiotics to combat the infection.

The cocktail of antibiotics resulted in a truly dangerous condition for Pam because she had recently become pregnant, although the doctors did not know it at the time. The placenta detached from the uterine wall, which deprived her baby of oxygen and the other essential nutrients that came from its mom. When the doctors discovered that she was pregnant, they immediately stopped the treatment, but they informed Pam that the baby had already been damaged.

Her "best" option, and maybe her only good option, said the doctor, was to terminate the pregnancy.

Bob and Pam were strong in their faith. They had given their lives to share the gospel in a cross-cultural environment halfway around the world from their Florida roots. No matter how logical or practical it sounded, they would not abort their baby. There was a God big enough to handle this problem. Their faith was rooted in the fact that they believed their God would intervene, and He did.

Pam went on bed rest at the hospital in her seventh month and remained on bed rest until August 14, 1987. Timmy was born a little malnourished, but in a very short time God made him healthy and well. Very healthy and very well to be exact.

Timmy went on to be a star quarterback at his high school. From there, he received an athletic scholarship to the University of Florida, where he helped lead his team to two national championships. As only a sophomore in college he was awarded the Heisman Trophy in 2007, which is given to the most outstanding college football player in the nation. Timmy was chosen in the first round of the NFL draft by the Denver Broncos, where he would eventually lead his team to the playoffs.

Aren't you glad Pam Tebow didn't abort her son, Tim? That's the story of Tim Tebow.

Abortion really isn't a political issue; it is a moral issue. My state, California, performs more abortions in America every year than any other state. Even in the midst of the worldwide pandemic of 2020 and 2021, Governor Gavin Newsom felt that abortion-on-demand was an essential business during the Covid-19 pandemic. So while small businesses, restaurants, churches, and mom and pop shops everywhere were closed, abortion clinics were deemed essential and therefore were fully open for business. (Loud sigh.)

I always admire those who stand outside of the abortion clinics and pray. There are some who volunteer weekly to peacefully try to engage young mothers, reminding them that there are other alternatives for their child than termination.

Furthermore, I think it is spectacular every year when churches post tiny crosses in their front yard to represent the lives of unborn children who were aborted. Those crosses preach a sermon to everyone who drives by that yard without ever speaking a word.

According to 2018 CDC data, 614,820 babies were aborted in America. Just for perspective, in 2020 there were approximately 393,000 Covid-19 related deaths in our country. Did you catch the numbers? Go back a few sentences and look at them again: More humans were killed in their mother's womb than died of Covid-19 in America in 2020! It seems the greatest threat to human life in 2020 was not Covid-19; it was the likes of Planned Parenthood and abortion clinics in general. Maybe we focused on the wrong pandemic.

Since the anniversary of Roe v. Wade, that fateful decision that was passed down on January 22, 1973, more than 61 million babies have been aborted in America.[1] That is sobering, sickening and saddening. Some people's lives are so important that we will shutter entire economies and countries to preserve them, while other people's lives are expendable.

---

1 Ertelt, S. (2020, January 10). 61,628,584 Babies Have Been Killed in Abortions Since Roe v. Wade in 1973. https://www.lifenews.com/2020/01/10/61628584-babies-have-been-killed-in-abortions-since-roe-v-wade-in-1973/.

I realize that if this book travels very far at all, there will be some reading who have had an abortion at one time in your life, maybe a couple. My heart hurts for you, and for what must go through your mind while journeying with us. First, I want you to know that there is no judgment here, not in the least. Let him who is without sin throw the first stone (see John 8:7). There is a God in heaven who knew about that moment, about that decision, and He loves you and He will forgive you if you will only ask.

Let me say this clearly so that we can connect on the deepest of levels. It absolutely breaks my heart to think about the millions of babies that have been aborted since 1973. I respect the churches who recognize Sanctity of Life Sunday, but if I'm honest, that is not enough. Anyone can identify problems; we make a difference when we offer solutions to the problems, and then participate in those solutions.

I am not the brightest crayon in the box, so that's why it seems like a no-brainer! If you are against abortion, then there are NO OTHER OPTIONS. You must be pro-foster. Excellent! We agree! Pro-life = Pro-Foster! Abortion is bad, Life is good. (Dude, if we continue to connect on this level, we might become besties.)

So, here is the 64-million-dollar question: What is your plan for those babies who don't get aborted?

What should we do with all of those children whose teenage moms were talked into giving birth? Do you have the picture in your mind yet? Let me lay it out for us just to make sure.

You and I are standing on the street in front of Planned Parenthood. We are peaceful and prayerful. After a few moments, we see a teenage girl get out of the car, her head down. Shame is causing her to hide under her oversized hoodie.

Suddenly, a miracle happens! We engage in a conversation, and the Holy Spirit gives victory. We aren't walking on water, but something miraculous happens. By the grace of God, we are able to love a young girl enough to help her understand that she is carrying a child! After several moments, maybe an hour, she changes her mind—NO ABORTION! Can I get a *woot woot*? Not today Satan!!!

A life is saved, and she carries her healthy baby full-term. We are so pumped! We begin to hashtag what we are feeling at that moment: #Godisgood #abortionisnottheanswer #lifeissaved #God1Satan0!

We give praise reports in church and our small group looks on us as if we have some sort of superpowers! All of our social media feeds are ablaze with our praise to God! Our feed is liked and shared by Christian social media influencers, and maybe it even goes viral in the faith-based community.

Full of hope and encouragement, we drive to the birthing center, talk our way back to the room, and bring our young friend some balloons. We talk about how amazing she is. We tell her that she will never regret this decision. We hug and cuddle and coo with a precious baby.

Then what? We hand the baby back, but our young friend is torn. She loves the baby, but she still has her whole life in front of her, right? She's still in high school. She has a geometry test on Tuesday and a civics quiz that she needs to make up when she returns to class. She loves this baby, but the reality of being a mom at sixteen young years of age is too much for her. Her parents can't care for the baby; they need to work. So, the girl goes to a fire station or a safe haven, and she surrenders her baby in a safe environment to the appropriate person.

So what happens to the baby? Where does it go? What next? The state steps in and Child Welfare Services takes the baby. Then what?

Social workers frantically network and find a home in which to place the child temporarily until a home can be identified for a long-term fostering-to-adopt solution. So here we are at Ground Zero. We talk the young mom into keeping the baby, and then we turn our heads when the child needs to be fostered and adopted. It's like we are ambivalent to what just happened. Someone pass me the blinders so I don't see my part in the solution, right?

What is your plan for those un-aborted youth? There is NO OTHER OPTION—it is foster care! Yes, there are social programs and agencies that can help with the needs of the child, but let's put this down on the bottom shelf so that anyone can access it. That child needs a place to go immediately to get food, a warm bed and a parent figure to help them to navigate the choppy seas of life. That's where foster parents come in!

Our First Placement

Here's a confession: we love what we do! Seriously, we really do—most of the time. You may think we're crazy, and we have certainly been called much worse, but we really love what we do.

Here's another confession: On the day when Dawn called me and said that we were going to have our first placement, the first thing that went through my mind was, "Will I be able to sleep with someone in our home who I barely know?" Our first placement was one of those "dreaded" teenagers.

We have had had teens in our home before. We had been youth pastors for 16 years when we decided to start fostering. Teens were nothing new to us, but we always knew the people who were sleeping near the knife drawer—know what I mean?

Never mind the fact that we had been through months and months of testing, screening, and even psychological evaluations. The process to be approved to be foster parents was long and arduous, but we were determined in our mission. We were excited.

Our first placement was a 17-year-old gangsta girl who was obviously gender confused. She was a girl who identified as a boy, walked as a boy and shopped in the boys' clothing section. Because we were short-term foster care providers, we didn't get a lot of information—only that she had a bit of a record, and that she was going to be aging out of the system in a little while.

At that moment the rubber met the road. If I am really pro-life, I must be pro-foster care. So bring it on, baby!

The first time I laid eyes on her, I saw that she looked like any other teen we had served for the better part of two decades. She was stocky, tatted, and had obviously been a member of a gang in a previous period of her life. Although I don't like to admit it, she might have been able to bench press more than me! (Maybe.)

While I'm confessing, here's another one: After I met her, I wondered if I would awaken the next morning spray-painted orange and duct-taped to the bed! I could just see myself being awakened in the night, our new friend standing over us in our bed with a knife from our kitchen, while we, that is Dawn, was screaming for her life. (Don't laugh, my vivid imagination is a very real part of my simple life.)

Smile, laugh, or just shake your head, but that was what actually went through my mind. Please be assured that nothing like that happened. In fact, nothing out of the ordinary happened.

She stayed with us for a month. She took Easter photos with our family. She willingly participated on a church construction project. She joined the family on a trip to Six Flags. Our fears were unfounded. We had an amazing time with her until she aged out on her 18th birthday.

Hundreds of Great Times

In a book about fostering, I suppose it would make sense to only write about the success stories, the wins, the times when we saw that we were making a difference. That would sell books. That would make everyone feel better about life.

But to be honest, there have been some not-so-fun days along the way. We knew most of what we were getting into; we were not caught off guard. So yes, there have been some challenges along the way.

We have battled and defeated head lice on both occasions it was brought into our home. Dawn's new iPhone was thrown in the toilet! (Yes, they really are water resistant.)

One of our trash cans has been "accidentally" set on fire, and no one seemed to know how it happened. Hundreds of dollars disappeared with one of our teenage young men. (That kid should go to Vegas and show the world his ability to make things disappear; Shin Lim has nothing on him.)

Both of us have been in aggressive situations with young people who were triggered into an unhealthy frame of mind. We have had children self-harm in our home. (Did you know that some teens will eat glass when they are triggered? We didn't either. We do now.) Probably not a highlight day in our journey.

We also know the power of the pot-laced "magic brownies" that get passed around at the junior high schools in our city. It will sadden you to know that even in junior high schools there is a drug cartel that control the "goods" that come in and out of the schools.

We have been investigated because a three-year-old accused us of spanking her; what a coincidence that this allegation came on a visit with her mom. (No, we do not spank). That could have been our most scary moment. It happened, we made it through and bought the t-shirt.

We have had police, fire trucks, EMT's, and safety personnel at our house several times. Our neighbors appreciate the break in the monotony of their otherwise quiet lives.

We have confronted adult predators who have tried to engage with an underage girl in our home. I would like to tell you it was Dawn's momma-bear complex and my bulging pythons that rippled from under my short-sleeved shirt that repelled the thugs! I would like to tell you that, but most probably it was just our unrelenting presence and our involvement that averted further danger to the children. (More on Dawn's momma-foster-bear superpower later, she's legit!)

Of our 36 placements and counting, several have run away. Some walked right out the front door daring us to try to stop them. Others opened the window, kicked out the screen and made their getaway in a more destructive fashion.

Although we have never felt unsafe, we have confiscated knives, bongs and various other drug paraphernalia. We found our daughter's underwear in the possession of one of our teenage foster sons.

We have even had both of the teen foster girls who were in our house run away at the same time, one from her school and one from our house! Try explaining that one to the sheriff's office: "Yes, officer, we need to file two reports for two of our foster girls who ran away from separate places at about the same time." God only knows what the dispatch officer must have thought after taking the call. You can't make this stuff up!

There you go. There it is. That is the reality. Some good stories, some bad stories, but as best as I can tell, the best alternative for abortion is fostering. We are presently fostering—still in the thick of things. There are some not-so-fun times for sure, especially during the global pandemic of 2020 that shut the schools down.

But for all of those "bad" memories, there are hundreds of shared joyful memories. We have been able to share life with some amazing young people. Maybe their lives are better now for their time in our home. Time will tell for sure.

We have been there for some children's first words! Priceless.

We have cheered at basketball games for children whose parents have never seen them play. We have watched wrestling matches and tried to talk intelligently about them on the car ride home. We have observed karate tournaments. (Did you know those were all-day events?)

We have sat at skate parks, and I now know how to dialogue about the difference between Ollie-flips and hard-flips!

We have seen kids united with their biological grandparents, and we have even been able to foster a little guy long enough to help him to get adopted into a Christian home! That was like winning the Super Bowl.

We have been at it just long enough to see kids settle down and relax, knowing that they won't get hit anymore. We have received good-night hugs. Some of our previous fosters even reach out and keep in touch! How cool is that?

On Mother's Day, 2019, Dawn received a call on her cell from the Santa Barbara Juvenile Detention facility. On the other end of the phone was a young man who wanted to wish Dawn (the closest thing to a mom he had) a Happy Mother's Day. (Why are my eyes watering right now?)

One of our greatest achievements was talking a young teenage girl through her decision to give birth to her baby by going full-term. She would later ask us if we would take her baby and raise it for her.

Just last week we received a text from a foster girl who aged out of the system. She informed us that she has a job, a bank account, an identification card, and she went on to say, "I'm adulting quite well if I do say so myself! You were the best parents I ever had." We only had her 3 months. Home run, touch 'em all baby!

Put a price on that! Nope, you can't. It's priceless.

On one occasion I pulled up to the local Krispy Kreme (pause for some heavenly music to warm our hearts together). I went into the store and this kid behind the counter yelled, "Jon!" I looked up and I recognized him immediately. He came out, hugged me, and asked if he could take his picture with me. Before it was all over I walked out with some free doughnuts! Now, if that isn't reason enough to do foster care, PRAY TELL, WHAT ARE YOU WANTING IN LIFE?

So, you're pro-life, and you are coming to understand that you are also pro-foster! I hope that you are able to see that being pro-foster is pro-rewarding!

We all agree that abortion is a terrible option, but so few think about the next logical step of care for the children. Who will foster the babies that we rescue from Planned Parenthood?

Have you ever thought about it? Why not you? Why haven't you thought of fostering before? Some of you have been thinking about it for a while. Why haven't you jumped in the pool yet? Hey, right here at the beginning of the book, if you feel that God is putting fostering on your heart—lean into it. God made you to love others, even if they don't love you back as much as you love them. Foster care really isn't about your heart, it's about the heart of fatherless children.

I have never met Brian Mavis, but he is the president of America's Kids Belong. I recently read one of his posts on Facebook. "Sometimes people ask me why I pursued orphan and foster care. My reply is 'I didn't. I pursued Jesus, and He led me to kids who needed families.'" Drop the mic, take a bow, and walk off the stage, sir! Well played, Mr. Mavis, well played.

What if Brian is right? What if pursuing Jesus is a journey that leads us into the brokenness of orphans and foster children? It has been for us, and I am so encouraged when I see Christ followers reaching out with compassion for the most needy among us.

That is why we are writing. I am not on a writing sabbatical. Dawn is not on a leave of absence from our two Intensive Services Foster Children. We are talking, journaling, researching and writing while juggling life because the need is so great.

There are children who, of no fault of their own, have been removed from their biological family and have been taken as wards of the state. The longing in their heart is the basic longing of every child: to have someone to love them.

Fostering at its very core is simply being a parent for someone else's children. Chances are you will never get spray-painted orange, but there is a good chance that you could change the trajectory of a life forever. Some of you are built to foster one child or one sibling set until they age out of the system. Some of you might be like us, and you can stand in the gap for some parents until the state can figure out what is the next best step. Either way, that is what we will do if we are pro-life. Pro-Life = Pro-Foster.

Discussion Questions

1. When the politician told Jon that churches spend more time and energy bashing abortion than they do supporting healthy options for moms and their children, did that hit home with you? What community causes have you engaged in that would aid the cause of the pro-life movement?

2. Why would it have been so easy and socially acceptable for Pam Tebow to have terminated her pregnancy? What would you say to those moms who carried their baby full-term, but their baby was born with serious health defects that will not allow them to enjoy a normal life?

3. Some might argue that if kids have to grow up in a bad life situation, it might be better for them to be terminated. What would you say to that contemporary line of thinking?

4. Jon and Dawn have spent most of their fostering journey with teens. Would you prefer to foster teens or younger children? Why?

5. What were the most exciting things about the positive shared times that Jon mentioned in this chapter? Would you agree that the joys of fostering outweigh the challenges?

6. Even if you don't become a mission-minded foster parent, what are some things you can do to support the pro-life and the pro-foster movement?

CHAPTER 3

Instant Crazy Family, the New Norm

Missional fostering is establishing a new norm for your family.

The film *Instant Family* is a brilliant and surprisingly accurate microcosm of what fostering family life looks like. In the movie, Mark Wahlberg and Rose Byrne play Mr. and Mrs. Wagner, a well-to-do couple with a nice home and empty bedrooms.

As Ellie, the wife, began to research foster children online, her heart melted. This led to the couple attending foster training and a picnic to see what foster kids are really like.

Before the picnic, they agreed that they should foster a younger child, because younger children are so adorable. While at the picnic, they encounter a feisty and defiant teenager who opens their eyes to the often-neglected teenagers in the foster care system. When they enquire into the possibility of opening their home to the teen, they find out that she has two younger siblings. Of course, no one wants to split up a family, so they agree to take in all three children.

I don't want to spoil the movie, and they sure aren't giving me any royalties, so all I'm going to say is this: They do get their instant family, but from that moment on, life gets crazy. Crazy with a hint of normal.

INSTANT CRAZY FAMILY FOR SURE!

When you take the plunge into the foster-care pool, be very certain that there will be ripples and waves. Maybe someone on the outside of the pool will even get a little bit wet. This needs to be said, so I will say it with a smile on my face (trust me it's there): Most foster youth are living in utter chaos, like when a tornado is bearing down on a farmhouse in Oklahoma. These children need some normal in their lives. But let me go on record here: when you bring a foster child into your home, your family dynamic will add an element of crazy. That is when you remember the reason missional foster parents get into the pool is because kids are drowning and their needs trump ours.

When we cannon-balled into fostering, we went all-in with the most challenging sector. God had called us, so we grabbed each other's hand, got a running start, and "launched into the deep end." Whatever normal our family had went out like last night's table scraps. We went from being the home that everyone on the block trusted because "that's the preacher's house" to being the house with all of the drama because "that's the foster house." Early on, families on the street would stop by to get me to pray for them; now they stop by to tell us they are praying for us! Crazy with a hint of normal is the new norm for missional foster parents.

I used to tell people that our house was a drug-free zone. I now say, "It is *supposed to be* a drug-free zone." One day, one of our foster teens posted a live video on her social media. One of our bio kids saw the video in which she was smoking marijuana in our house—a.k.a the preacher's house! That was the first time I heard of "puff bar;" it was not our last time. For us, that was crazy.

And then there were the occasional weapons, because one of the young men would make knives out of scrap metal in his welding class at school and bring them home. As long as he was in our home we would pat him down every day when he walked in the door from school. That became our new normal—a crazy normal.

Although there were house rules, our home began to be decimated with profanity: "F-this" and "F-that." (I had really no idea of how many combinations of F-words there were until we began fostering, but apparently it can be used in almost any sentence.)

Before you go all "Judge Judy" on us, of course we had house rules, but having rules and getting young ones to respect those rules are separate issues. Now, we have learned to charge them $1.00 when they F-bomb around us. You would be surprised how quickly things can become G-rated.

If you stop to think about it, crazy is the norm that foster kids know. Crazy life is the only life they have grown up in. It is what they experience day-in and day-out. Different men in and out of momma's bedroom. Long periods of time with no one to get them food or change their diapers or help them to get the cereal off of the top shelf. We once caught a one-year-old toddler climbing the pantry shelves to fend for herself because that was what she was used to doing when she got hungry. That was her crazy normal.

Illegal substances, hangovers, and fighting: that is their reality. There is a reason that children are in foster care! Crazy is normal to them, so whatever drama happens when they enter your home is like a Sunday-school picnic to them. They have seen, heard, and navigated some Class 5 rapids, so when they go all ballistic on you, remember that they have learned that behavior and heard those words by observing their parents and others close to them.

Do you have eyes that allow you to see past the behaviors and beyond the surface? Missional foster parents can—maybe not at first, but with some on-the-job training it will happen. It takes a little bit of time, but you will find yourself asking questions like these: "What is causing this behavior? What are they really trying to say? What is going on way down behind those cute little eyes of yours? What are you thinking? What scared you? What triggered you?"

On more than one occasion foster kids in our house have said things like, "I just want to be like the other kids and be normal." Fosters come to realize that their life is not normal, and somewhere along the way, many of them come to believe that they are not normal.

Fosters want a normal home that is free from social workers, forever! Other kids don't have a social worker, so why should they? They want a normal where their mom and dad aren't in trouble with the law every weekend. They want a normal life where they don't have to go to family court. Foster youth want to go to school and not get pulled out of class every other day for appointments with therapists and mental health specialists. In short, foster youth crave what your family has and probably takes for granted.

Fosters want to live in a home where they don't have to play the parent. They know it is not the norm to parent their parents and their younger brothers and sisters. Oldest children in the sibling set will often function as the parent in your home because that is what they have been doing for as long as they can remember.

Fostering is about seeing a mission and operating with a wartime mentality. There are some kids who are living in homes that look like war-torn Baghdad. Crazy is what they live day-in and day-out, and it is now part of the baggage that they will bring into your home. They really do want to be in a normal family, but in the process of blending your lives together, your normal becomes more crazy and their normal becomes less crazy.

"Mom and Pops"

Molly was beautiful, funny, smart, talented, and an excellent reader. She was 15, she looked like Lindsey Lohan, and she had incredible personality and natural charm.

When I walked in the door and saw someone as attractive as her sitting at our table, I was shocked. We came to find out that we were her thirty-third foster home! (Pause and let the number 33 sink in.) That's right, she had been removed from her mother early in life, and over the short 15 years of her lifetime, she had called 33 different addresses her home. She had essentially moved an average of 2 times per year, every year of her life. Our hearts went out to her.

Molly quickly meshed with Dawn and I. Somehow, someway we found her breaking down the walls around our personal spaces and conquering our hearts like a Roman emperor in AD 70. She was fun-loving and she actually seemed to embrace our parenting talks in the beginning. She wanted the structure, the attention, the rules. It made her feel loved.

As foster parents we practice a hands-off policy because we never know if a child has been touched inappropriately, so we allow any contact to be initiated from them. Molly gave us hugs at night before she went to bed. She would knock on our bedroom door in the morning to give us a hug before she got on the bus. She was loving the family, and we were loving her.

I will never forget one of her first nights at our home, she asked what she should call us. I told her that many of the fosters called me "The Supreme Commander." (That is truth—I definitely told her that, but it is not true that many of the fosters ever called me The Supreme Commander.) She laughed warmly and asked if she could call us "Mom and Pops."

What do you say to that? Y-E-A-H! Of course you can! I gotta tell you, that warmed our hearts in a way like I simply cannot explain with words. One of the pre-agreed upon goals Dawn and I had when we went into fostering was to consider adopting a teenager who would mesh with our family, one that we could give a forever home. So when Molly looked into my eyes and called me "Pops," my defenses were down, my heart was smitten, and I was ready to meet with the family court judge and make it official!

Molly was polite and respectful. She loved going live on Insta as she and I would drive in the car. She was posting about her "parents" and how cool her dad was when he would take her to get maple doughnuts from Krispy Kreme. When we would get in the car, she would find *The Greatest Showman* soundtrack on my phone, and then within seconds it would be playing on the Bluetooth: Hugh Jackman in all of his glory, belting it out to anyone within a half-mile of our car.

I enjoyed the relationship we were having. She loved being in a "normal" family (her words, not mine).

I remember driving her to spend some time at her biological relatives' home. That was the first time I heard her say, "My family is so screwed up. Everybody always fights, and my mom doesn't get along with any of her family." Then, with a quiver in her voice she said, "All I ever wanted was a normal family."

No matter how many times I tried to encourage her, we both knew it was not normal to bounce around 32 times. CWS had stepped into her life from the very beginning, so to Molly, all she had ever known was foster care, and she was tired of it. To this day I can still hear those words, "All I ever wanted was a normal family." To fosters, normal is drama-free. Normal is loving and predictable. Normal homes don't need the police to come and sort things out. If my guess is right, then your home would qualify as a normal home.

It is for Molly, and for the hundreds of thousands of others like her, that we write. What did Molly do wrong? Nothing.

Her only problem is that she was born to a young, teenage mom who thought she could provide a good home life for her child. There are Mollys everywhere, in every county and in every state. So, for Mollys everywhere, we ask, is there any chance you might have a bit of room in your life to help someone feel like all the other kids? You know—normal.

What Is a Normal Family?

Normal has nothing to do with the neighborhood in which you reside. Normal is not a reference to the square footage of your house or the number of shared bathrooms you have. Normal is not about your age as a foster parent or whether or not you have a dog. When fosters say "normal," they are implying things like stability, security, attention, and love.

All kids are sensitive to norms around them. Fosters realize that they spend a lot of time going to and from court. Sometimes fosters have to take meds to help them regulate, but they notice that most other kids don't. Foster youth come to realize that their parents have addictions, ankle monitors, and probation officers. One teenage boy said of his mom, "I don't like the way she dresses, because it makes my friends talk about her." When a boy's friends talk about his mom in an inappropriate way, that is not normal.

When Molly said she wanted to be in a "normal" family, she would follow it up with, "My family is so screwed up." So, let's finish this chapter with a dialogue about what "normal" really is. This list is not rocket science. These are not skills that can only be acquired at an Ivy League school. You don't need to get your Masters degree or even your GED. Some of the most helpful things we can do are actually some of the most common things we can do.

Questions

1. Will you use your foster as a punching bag when they mess up something in your home?

2. Will you use the rent money to pay for drugs?
3. Will you leave the fosters in your care unattended and locked in their rooms until you return?
4. Will you let strangers come into your home to have conjugal visits with you or your mate so you can make money?
5. Will you give the kids baths and take videos and post them online for money?
6. Will you and your mate get stoned out of your mind on weekends, leaving open beer cans and pill bottles laying around?
7. Will you go into your children's rooms at night to pleasure yourself?
8. Will you yell at the fosters the way they yell at you?
9. Will you gamble away all the foster kid's food money?

Yeah, I know that was offensive, but that is their normal! That is where they are coming from. If you answered NO to all of those questions, you have a "normal" that is better than the craziness they are coming from.

Is it possible that you are exactly what the doctor would order for some underserved children? I'll bet it is not only possible—I'll bet it is probable!

You can be a part of creating a new normal for someone who has only known crazy. I believe in you. I am convinced you can do it. Instant crazy family could be one of the most exciting chapters of your life.

Think about it. Pray about it . . . but keep reading.

Discussion Questions

1. For those who have seen the film *Instant Family*, share your feedback about how the movie affected you. If you haven't seen it, google "Instant Family trailers" and you can watch a short trailer to pique your interest.

2. In your own words, describe how Jon and Dawn's home changed as soon as they opened up their home to short-term foster children. In what ways do you think it stretched them? How do you think it solidified the commitment to their mission?

3. What do you think goes through a foster youth's mind when they have to be a parent to their parents or to their younger brothers and sisters?

4. What do you think Molly was enjoying at Jon and Dawn's home that looked like "normal"?

5. Read back through the 9 questions at the end of this chapter and describe the abnormal living condition that is implied in each scenario.

CHAPTER 4

Our Story

Missional fostering. How did we get here?

I would like to tell you that before we got married we had committed that we were going to get into fostering. Like I said, I would like to tell you that, but that wouldn't be accurate. Our story did not involve angelic visions or dreams at night of helping fatherless kids. I would like to tell you we read the Bible, saw all of the references to the fatherless children and that is what motivated us, but truthfully it was none of those.

Here's how it happened for us.

Dawn's Story

I always knew that I was meant to help kids. As a child, I dreamed of working in an orphanage one day. I was thrilled when my parents became foster parents when I was in junior high school. Over the years, my parents cared for several children and adults through social services, but they also cared for dozens of others by their loving hospitality and opening their homes to those in need.

Almost all of my memories include extra people around the dinner table or extended family members sleeping in my bed while I camped out in my little brother's room. When the neighbor's house burned down, the single dad and 3 kids lived with us for 9 months while their house was being rebuilt. When my dad's youngest brother needed a place to stay, he moved in with us for several months. One young man parked his camper in our yard for a semester while he studied at the local college, and he ate many meals with us. All these situations helped prepare me for a future of hospitality and willingness to open my home to strangers and guests.

Fast forward several years, I meet Jon.

I remember mentioning my desire to foster and/or adopt to Jon before we were married and several times through the early years of our marriage. After marriage, we were crazy busy in our careers, ministries, and child-rearing. So, although I had occasional thoughts of fostering or adopting, it wasn't anything I talked to Jon about. It simply was not the time. However, as our kids got into elementary school, I started thinking about it more often.

I would voice these thoughts to Jon once or twice a year over the next decade, something like this: "I just want to let you know that I think about fostering kids all the time. If you every have a desire to do that, I'm extremely interested." Jon would say something like, "OK, maybe one day. I can't see how we can put anything else into our lives right now, though."

By the time our kids were in high school, I was pretty much consumed with the desire to foster. Privately, I researched all about foster kids and kids who were waiting to be adopted. If you've seen the film Instant Family, you remember Ellie crying in front of her computer screen as she saw all the children waiting for a home. That was me.

Hoping to give me a diversion, my husband, who is not fond of pets, let us get a dog. That actually helped for a couple years! But then, several things started to happen, but I'll let Jon tell you the rest of the story . . . he is ready to grab the mic from my hands anyway.

Jon's Story: "Too Busy"

Yeah, everything she just said is absolutely true. She is the one who championed the cause in our family. The next few paragraphs will disappoint you I'm sure, and I suppose they should.

Ok, let's go ahead and get this out of the way. I am the one who held us back from fostering for years. (*Loud gasp.*) Imagine this for a headline in the local paper: "The pastor of a church is the one who held his foot on the brake when it came to serving the neediest of our community." I can hear you hiss, but before you go all "Karen" on me, I just thought there was no way our schedule could take anything else. "God, we're already busy doing what You've called us to do."

Put simply, I just thought we were too busy. It wasn't that I was turning a deaf ear to these kids on purpose, but we were already working with kids. For the first 15 years of our marriage, we served as the youth pastor team at our church. Our youth group grew to over 100 every week. We were working with kids! Now that I look back on things, I can see that I made the issue about me. I justified my inactivity with foster children by looking at all of the things that I was already doing "for God."

I know, I know, wrong answer! My life is not about me. It never has been. It is about the One who lives inside of me. Christ in me was wanting to add another dimension to our ministry work—fatherless kiddos.

I think there are many good-hearted people who feel entirely incapable to do foster care because of their schedules. I get it. You volunteer in AWANA at your church, you rotate on the worship team, you host the weekly small group in your home, you are the team mom for all of your kids' soccer teams, you care for your aging parents, you have a gym membership and . . . Hey, I feel ya, I really do—that was how we felt.

Dawn and I had three biological children already, and all of them played at least two sports a year. And as best as I can tell, I almost never missed one of our children's ballgames! For a couple of years, I really did feel like our car was an Uber! After all, I was a pastor of a busy church. And a small group leader. And we hosted a youth meeting in our home every week. And did I mention that I was a chaplain for our sheriff's office as well? And then there were the cross-country trips we took to look after my parents. Translation: "Our lives are too busy for these kids. Let other people solve this problem; we can't do everything, ya know!"

"Surely there have to be other more qualified, less busy people than us! There must be a waiting list of empty nesters and adults who didn't have any kids, or maybe one or two kids, who have some time on their hands to foster. I'm positive that boatloads of God's people are standing in line to care for these young ones." That was the justification in my mind when Dawn would mention something about fostering . . . over the next 20 years! (*Audience gasps.*)

It is not that I didn't love people, it was just that I never really saw the fatherless' and orphans' true needs. I had a mission, and I was locked into my interpretation of what that mission would look like. I was already doing what God wanted. Would God change my mission orders?

Now we are at Ground Zero. Take a moment and reflect on this. It might explain your situation as well. God was in a box of my making, a box that after 25 years of serving as a pastor, I felt like I could control.

Additionally, I never saw the needs of the foster children that Dawn had been talking about. I had never stopped to think about what they were going through. I saw my needs, our needs, some other people's needs, the church needs, but not foster youths' needs.

Even if we could have / would have been exposed to the true depths of loss, poverty, and family brokenness in the youth in our county, I just couldn't see how our lives could take any more craziness. We were busy serving Jesus for Pete's sake! What more could God want of us?

Finally, God at Work in Me

The first time Dawn ever said "Hey, if you ever have any thoughts about fostering or adoption, I am open to it," I thought, "Who in the world was thinking that? Certainly not me, that's for sure!" Once a year for decades she would drip that line into our conversations. I am thankful she was gracious in the way she would bring it up. God was already at work in her heart. I was the weak link.

Well, as you can imagine because you are reading this book, God changed our lives and our mission for sure. Forever.

When our youngest son was going into ninth grade, I sat down with Dawn and told her that she had been a rock star for our family. She had set her career aside to raise our 3 children. With one of the children in college and the other two in high school, I thought it was the right time to see what she would like to do for fulfillment and meaning outside of our family. (Being an Enneagram #3, this was in keeping with the desire to win the Husband of the Year award.) I continued, "Do you want to go and get your Masters degree in music, or maybe take some additional classes at the local college for a current education certification? Whatever you want to do, just let me know." (That's what contestants in the Husband of the Year Competition say to their wives, ya know.)

She didn't need a lot of time to reply. She didn't begin with "Hmm . . ." I'm 100% positive I didn't see her bow her head to pray. It was like she had been waiting for the question. Her answer shook me to the very core: "Well, I think if I could do anything, I would like to foster." Ugh! Gulp! Gasp! I didn't see that one coming. That was certainly not on my radar. I wanted to add fostering children into our life like I wanted to add a root canal into next week's calendar! (Note to self, don't ask Dawn any more questions you don't already know the answer to!)

As much as I tried to defend my "We can't possibly do this because we are way too busy" position, I couldn't. I coughed, stammered, and said, "Wow, I didn't think that was what you would say." God had my attention, and He was using my wife to get it.

It didn't happen overnight, but the seeds that Dawn had been sowing for years began to come to life and puncture the soils of my heart, sending their tiny sprouts up through the softening layers of my mind.

First, God placed a lady in our life who had been through the foster system. That's the way God works: He weaves someone or some event into your life when you aren't expecting it. It was subtle, but effective. This book may very well be that for you. Maybe this is God's way of awakening desires that He has inserted into your life. Maybe He is illuminating something that has been in your mind a long time, a dream that has been tucked away on a shelf that you had forgotten was there. Paul said something to that effect in the second chapter of his book to the Philippians: "For it is God who works in you both to will and to do for His good pleasure" (v. 13).

She was a young Air Force sergeant named Infinity. She and her husband were stationed at the Air Force base near our church.

They began to attend our church, and one Sunday I asked her to share her life story in one of the services. I will never forget the day she stood on the stage and began to tell her story. To my utter amazement, it led to her telling us about her journey through the foster-care system. I was dumbfounded. Mesmerized.

She spoke of the hurt she experienced before she ended up with her grandmother. It was a tough road for her. To this very day I can still see her behind the lectern, a truly influential sister in Christ, redeemed by the blood of Jesus, standing in God's great grace, and proclaiming that she was thankful for the loving home that eventually pointed her to Jesus, who would become her Lord and Savior!

She had no idea that God was dealing with me as I was sitting there, mouth wide open, a lump in my throat and a knot in my stomach! I thought God would use her to encourage the church family, yet God used her to advance His new calling on our lives.

God was directing my heart into an area of mission that would not require us to move from our native country or learn a new dialect. God was not asking us to take the gospel to the forgotten and unreached people groups in the 1040 window. God was beginning to show us that there was a forgotten and unreached people group in our county that needed the love of Jesus. Imagine if we could display the love of God to children in our home as had happened with Infinity.

The plot was thickening. I never said anything to Dawn about what God was doing in me. It was too new, raw, and unfamiliar.

Meanwhile, second in God's cast of characters that He used to re-define our mission was a new friend at the coffee shop. Enter stage left, Larry (his real name). Larry showed up at my "Starbucks office" a couple of times a week. I am a people person and I love to spend my time studying at coffee shops, smiling, engaging with people. Every customer is a friend just waiting for us to connect—that is how I see it.

Here's how coffee-shop friendships happen. Some of you know exactly what I'm talking about. Nods turn into waves, which turn into pleasantries, which turn into conversations, which turn into friendships. It is brilliant (and sovereign) how God sneaks people into our lives that impact us, then *POOF,* they are gone, moved to another state!

Our friendship just happened organically, and like most men Larry and I talked of our hobbies (bike riding) and jobs. I told him that I was a pastor of the church down the street and he told me he was a rep for Pathways Foster Family Agency. When he said that, I almost spewed my Starbucks tall blonde out of my mouth! Are you kidding me?! "Did you say, 'Foster agency'? God, are you serious right now?"

During our conversations he told me about a short-term fostering plan in the state of California. When children are removed from their homes, the social workers need a home that can receive children in the spur of the moment and keep them until a semi-permanent home can be arranged with a family member or a long-term foster care home. I had never heard of this before. Fireworks began to go off inside my head!

Larry went on, "Think of it like triage: an emergency room to help to stop the bleeding and get the kids stabilized so that they can be evaluated and helped." Those words sounded to me like mission! Mission in the trenches. Real soul care. God's mission! God's mission for some needy kids! Gods mission for our family! "These kids usually stay a couple of weeks in that temporary home and then they transition out into a more permanent placement. When they move on, your home is opened back up to do the process all over again."

The juices were flowing. The Spirit was working. A change was a-comin' to our family for sure.

It took Ebenezer Scrooge three visions before he would change, and it took me three people as well. The last and probably the most influential of all of the characters in God's plan was the lady down the street. She will remain unnamed. She never actually showed up on the stage, but her words still ring like church bells at Christmastime.

Here's how it happened. Our youngest son was playing basketball with his friends. One of them was a foster child from down the street. Our son, Jason, invited the foster youth to come to the youth group meeting that night. The boy said, "I can't go. My (foster) mom doesn't believe in God, so we don't go to church or anything like that anymore." Our son relayed the sad story to me and that is when I yielded to God. Right there, on the spot. I raised the white flag: God won. If only non-believers foster children, then the hope of these children seeing or hearing Jesus as a child will be greatly diminished.

It wasn't about how bad this other foster mom was—she is actually an amazing lady who ended up adopting a sibling set of three! Without question she has been a huge encouragement to us on our journey, and if memory serves, she is a second-generation foster parent. We respect her greatly.

However, that moment was when God was able to peel the scales off of my eyes. Foster parents have a huge impact on their children! HUGE!

"Hi, this is your Captain speaking; we see turbulence in the next few sentences, please return to your seats and fasten the seat-belt firmly across your lap. Thank you." Are you ready for it? Here it comes . . .

If Christians don't have room in their lives for fatherless children, then WHAT IN THE WORLD ARE WE DOING? What are we doing that is so important that we are simply too busy to help hurting and needy children? Why wouldn't Christ followers bring foster kids into their home? That's what missional fostering is all about! What if you are supposed to foster just so that you can display the love of Christ for a child or teen who just might happen to see Jesus in you? My Christ-following brother and sister, what is your life about if not to live for missions like that?

"Hi, Captain Jon again. We have been told that the rest of the chapter will be smooth sailing. Thanks for flying with Missional Fostering. We will have you into the gate a bit early today."

I really do believe that Jesus is the answer to every question, the solution to every problem and the cure for every pandemic. Why wouldn't Christ followers model the love of God for kids who may or may not know what a good Father looks like? If Christ followers shut our doors to the children in the system, then WHO IN THE WORLD WILL TAKE THESE KIDS IN?

As I said earlier, you don't have to be a Christ follower to love kids. However, Christ followers have an added dimension to their love for people because Christ IN us is a game changer! Paul nailed it in his letter to the Colossians when he wrote: "Christ in you, the hope of glory" (Colossians 1:27). Christ can love kids through kind words, warm beds, and hot chocolate with marshmallows and sprinkles!

Not only does Christ live IN us, but He also fills our tanks with love for others through us. "And may the Lord make you increase and abound in love to one another and to all, just as we do to you" (1 Thessalonians 3:12). If you don't love the kid who just got dropped off at your home, no problemo amigo, Jesus will increase your love for others. Jesus is the source, the reservoir, the fountain head.

On the night before He was to offer up His life as a sacrifice for the world, Jesus uttered these words to a small group of his friends. "A new commandment I give to you, that you love one another; as I have loved you, that you also love one another. By this all will know that you are My disciples, if you have love for one another" (John 13:34-35).

Love others as He has loved us. That is a high bar—a very, very high bar.

Could I love a foster youth like Jesus would love that child if Jesus were living at my address? Yup! Why? Because Jesus is living in me, and Jesus can give me the love that I need in the moment it is needed.

After my son Jason told me of his conversation with his basketball friend, I knew what needed to be done. God had patiently been directing us into this mission for quite some time. I am grateful for His patience, but disappointed that it took me so long to jump into fostering.

I walked into the house and told Dawn that I believed that God had made it clear to me that we should probably start our paperwork toward becoming foster parents. I wish I could remember her reaction. Maybe she cried, maybe she kissed me, maybe she questioned my identity, or maybe she just thanked the Lord for His faithful work in our lives. Finally, her dream was becoming a reality and our home was becoming a missional foster family.

Living Proof

I am living proof that God can change hearts. I wasn't coerced or constrained to get into foster care. I was complicit with what God was doing. God changed my desires. My heart had caught up with Dawn's. We were both now *All In.*

This change in our family, mostly in me, is nothing short of what Paul said to the young churches in Galatia, "For He who worked effectively in Peter for the apostleship to the circumcised also worked in me toward the Gentiles" (Galatians 2:8).

God works in our hearts to do what He wants for us to do. That is beautiful. And grace-filled. And so God-like.

I hope that encourages everyone reading this book. Dawn and I are enlisted into the ranks of foster-care parents because God worked in our hearts to do it. We want the mission. We enlisted in the cause. We are in foster care because it is something that He wanted us to do, and consequently, that became what we want to do. Now we are encouraging you to jump in—the water is fine!

Maybe you are like me, a little unsure of the process. Or maybe you fear the commitment level. Maybe you are afraid that you don't have what it takes. Maybe you feel like you couldn't handle the pressure, or maybe you feel like you would screw things up if you were to get involved.

Rest easy my friend. God is the one who changes hearts and surgically implants His desires inside us. I like how David put it in Psalm 37:4: "Delight yourself also in the LORD, and He shall give (to) you the desires of your heart." Our job is to focus on Him, and His job is to get us doing His plan. The way He does that is through our desires.

God is the One who performs an extreme makeover on your "wanter" so that you will want to do what He wants you to do. God builds a dream somewhere in heaven's warehouse and then ships it to your heart, and over time the Holy Spirit begins construction on building that dream smack-dab in the middle of your passions and desires.

That is great stuff: If God wants you to foster, you will want to foster.

If you are reading this in a group session, make sure you share with your group what desires God is putting inside of you. If you are flying solo today, then make sure that before you leave the plane you take a moment to process the desires, thoughts, and interests that are awakening inside of you. Talk to your mate or your soulmate or to someone who can help you to discern God's hand in your life.

Happy talks lie ahead, you may unbuckle your seatbelt and proceed to the front of the plane. Our story is over. I wonder how many stories are just beginning.

In the next chapter, we want to fly over the Scriptures and see what, if anything, they say about fostering.

Discussion Questions

1. God prepared Dawn's heart for fostering in a different way than Jon's. Contrast their journeys. What encourages you about their story?

2. Respond to this sentence: "If Christians don't have room in their lives for fatherless children, then WHAT IN THE WORLD ARE WE DOING? Why wouldn't Christ followers bring foster kids into their home?" Wouldn't a home be a great place for Christ followers to display the love of Christ and the truth of the gospel?

3. In what ways is missional foster care an outflow of John 13:34-35? In what ways do foster parents display the love of God to children and their parents?

4. If God wants you to foster children, what would His plan look like? Build your answers around Psalm 37:4 and Galatians 2:8.

5. What are some of the things God is doing in your heart to serve fatherless children?

CHAPTER 5

Wanted

What I am going to tell you next is the truth, the whole truth, and nothing but the truth, so help me God. Our three bio kids will swear to it. What I am about to say could be proven in a court of law!

My wife is guilty. Here is her crime: Dawn has a favorite child!

The sheer amount of photos of him in her photo stream will convict her without a shadow of doubt. She is just like ol' Jacob from Hebrew history. She may not have given him a coat of many colors, but the evidence is overwhelming! Here's what will blow your mind: her fave is not a bio child! You read that correctly, no need to go back and re-read the last sentence—your first take was correct. Her favorite child did not come to us through my Y chromosome; he came to us through foster care, and his name is Shane.

Shane came to us as an emergency placement. I'm going to hand the mic to Dawn for a minute. This is her Facebook entry on Mother's Day 2020:

> *We had only been a shelter home for 2 months when Shane arrived. Seventeen months old, nonverbal, filthy, both eyes swollen with pink-eye, and terrified. He showed signs of emotional trauma*

such as rocking and head-banging and he had several developmental delays. But God allowed me to be his Mom-figure for 14 months.

As a shelter home, we typically get the children in emergency situations and for a short time while the authorities look to find a long-term foster home. After six grueling days with Shane, the social worker took him to a long-term placement, and Jon and I were very happy to get a full night of sleep! The next morning, however, we got a call that they were bringing him back. This poor traumatized toddler could not handle the trauma, so Shane returned! Little did we know that we were going to fall in love with this little guy and have him with us for the next 14 months!

Shane Enters Our Lives

Here's the story behind the post. He was nonverbal, had 6 digits on each hand, and had been severely neglected. Shane was one of two children removed from a young couple. Normally authorities try to keep sibling sets together, but in this case, both of the children needed so much care that it was deemed essential to split them up. God's providential hand was moving, although no one was aware of it at the time. Mission can do that to people, ya know. Mission can cause us to get so locked into the day-to-day triage that we fail to see a sovereign God who is carefully orchestrating the events of life in His time.

Shane's neglect was obvious to all. His extra digit had not been removed, and when he arrived at our home, he had pink-eye. Although we can't say for sure, we feel that he had spent much time alone, because he was unable to be left by himself for even a minute. If we would do so, he would rock his body and bang his head on the floor, which are textbook signs of neglect.

On his first night in our home, Dawn fed him, bathed him, and held him in her arms. She then tucked him into his crib, turned off the light and walked back into our family room. It was a job well done! She sat down on the couch beside me and let out a happy sigh of fatigue. She was in her happy place with a little one in our home again.

Wait, What? He's Out!

What happened next I will never in a million years forget. We heard a noise from his bedroom, then the sound of something like a doorknob, and after that little bare feet in the hallway behind us. JAILBREAK! Shane bolted out of the room with eyes opened wide as if to say, "Did you guys realize you left me in that room all by myself? I'm sure it was an oversight—no problem, we will put this behind us. Hey, what's on TV?!?" He simply could not handle being left alone in a room by himself.

No, we are not making this up! Nothing is being embellished!

Now what? How in the world were we ever going to sleep? What if he just walked right out of the house into the street? Dawn slept that night outside of his room so that if he tried to get out, he would have to crawl over her. The next morning we encouraged each other with the good news that this was a short-term assignment. It *was* a short-term assignment, right? Of course, that's what we had signed up for, short-term placements; we just needed to hold things together until the social workers could get things sorted out.

Those six days were challenging. We couldn't turn our backs for a moment. He was different from our bios; they had received attachment and attention, so they were able to exist for short periods of time when we needed to step out of the room for hydration or elimination. Shane, not so much. Now that he had our attention, he was probably fearful we would desert him as well.

Sunday came around, so we took Shane to church with us and checked him into the nursery. To be honest, it brought back fond memories of doing so with our own children. Walking into church with a young guy was a rush, I'm not going to lie. We reasoned that this must be the way grandparents feel when they strut around with their grandchildren. Everyone was fawning over this little guy, and they had good cause—he was a cutie!

By the time Dawn picked him up at the end of the service it was obvious that things didn't go well. Apparently the other kids in the nursery were not quite as fond of him as we were. He had beaten up all of the sweet girls in their beautiful dresses and he had pulled the hair of the nursery worker who tried to hold him. I'm pretty sure we might have lost a family or two from our church that week. "Good thing our foster care is of the short-term variety," we told ourselves.

I will confess that it was a bit of a relief when the social worker called and informed us that Shane would be gone by the end of the next day. Sure enough, within a matter of hours he was gone into the loving arms of a family who was interested in fostering a child long-term. Mission accomplished, or so we thought.

Wait, What? He's Back!

Within 12 hours Dawn's phone rang again. It was our social worker. Shane was coming back! The family that had him one night said they just couldn't handle him. Since he knew us a little bit, they were bringing him back to our home. That was not the happiest moment in our life, but this time we were going to be ready.

Game on little guy! This go-around Dawn was prepared: she installed baby monitors with a video camera and armed the door with a child safety lock so he couldn't escape in the night when everyone was sleeping. Shane's bedroom had the makings of a Supermax facility for toddlers! This time we were ready—bring it on Shane! What we weren't quite ready for was how this little guy would wiggle his way into our hearts forever.

As I looked back over our photo library, I noticed that for the first 30 days I didn't take any pictures of the little guy. Dawn snapped a few and she had some cute videos, but not many.

One month turned into two. We started snapping cute pictures as he made us laugh. Shane responded well to structure, nurture, and care. At first we were surprised that the system wasn't moving him, and the only thing that we could get from the social workers was that when prospective long-term foster care families would read his file they'd pass on him.

Their loss! This boy was beginning to relax, adjust, adapt, and thrive in our home. We took more pictures: Shane eating ice cream; Shane dumping his Cheerios on the floor and eating them; Shane cuddling with our son, Jason; Shane wearing my sunglasses; Shane riding in the convertible with his hands up. Shane was the Boss Baby, large and in-charge!

On a grander scale, God was doing something, but He wasn't looping us in just yet. We stayed on mission, and this mission was getting more and more enjoyable every day we did life with Shane. Jesus once said something that applies to our mission of following Him when He said, "No one, having put his hand to the plow, and looking back, is fit for the kingdom of God" (Luke 9:62). Our role in this story was on the very bottom shelf—to keep our eyes focused on what God had called us to do—be a foster parent.

Two months turned into three, and three into four. The longer he stayed, the more we began to fall for the little guy, and the more photos we took: More pictures of Shane with sunglasses; Shane in the convertible again; Shane on the playground; Shane sleeping; Shane eating—Shane, Shane, Shane!

Our son who was in college in Florida would call, and Shane would utter loud gibberish into the phone. Shane was fully engaged in the conversation, as if my son had called to talk to him! Our other two bios began to fall for him as well. By the time the 6-month mark came around we were no longer asking how long he would be staying; we were shamelessly hinting to the social workers that we should just leave him here (in our "short-term" home) until they found out what would be happening to him, *wink wink*. We had fallen for him hook, line, and sinker!

Meanwhile, Shane's sister was thriving in her foster home with her new family. The Lopez family, who already had two children under the age of three, were seriously considering adopting Shane's little sister, but the state wanted to keep the sibling set together. If the Lopez family were to adopt Shane's sister, then it was a package deal, and the boy with 12 digits was absolutely included in the package deal.

Secretly we began to pray that the Lopez family would adopt both Shane and his sister. I think that was the first time we began to catch a glimpse of what our Father might be doing. We had not received any "Top Secret" emails from any of the members of the Trinity, but we have known our Father for decades now, and sometimes we as believers can begin to see His hands at work. We stayed on the mission He had assigned to us and prayed. Dawn took more videos and photos.

We loved Mr. and Mrs. Lopez right from the start. We loved the way they doted on their children, and we loved that they shared our faith in God. We felt confident that if Shane could grow up in that home, he would hear the good news of the gospel at a young age. We were also sure that they would love him to pieces as well. The obvious difficulty for the Lopez family was having four children under the age of 5, three of them under the age of 3! We prayed, hoped, and trusted that God was at work. Then we took some more photos and videos of Shane.

About that time, the biological grandmother stepped in and secured a very savvy lawyer so that she could try to adopt the children. She couldn't bear the thought of losing her bio grandchildren. Our hearts broke for her every time we would see her at court. (Being a foster parent doesn't mean that we are against the biological family in any way. Truly, much ministry work can be done when we reach out with loving arms and compassionate hearts to the bio family.) We empathized with her and prayed for our Father to do what was best for those children.

I suppose that there is a temptation to look down on parents who have their children removed. "Obviously you screwed things up; good thing I'm here to fix this child." That is so far from the gospel message. The gospel says that we are all broken and that there is a Hero who has good news for us! Humility is the robe of the Spirit-filled foster parent. The apostle Paul was spot-on when he wrote, "But by the grace of God I am what I am" (1 Corinthians 15:10).

The facts of the case should not be aired in this format, but as much as we felt the grief of the bio grandmother, we felt convinced that Shane would be better served with the Lopez family. It hurts to remember the grandma's tears; we do not envy the family court judges who reside over these cases. The judge had previously terminated the rights of both of the biological parents, so the only biological relative who still had any rights at the time was this grandma.

By now, Shane had been with us for more than a year. He was in our family Christmas photos with a little electronic "blotch" on his face to protect his identity on social media. Long-term care is not what either of us had signed up for, but this little guy was now deeply rooted in our hearts, and the same was true for Mr. and Mrs. Lopez. Dawn and Mrs. Lopez began to arrange play dates for Shane so that he could interact with his little sister and with their family. Slowly but surely, God began to knit Shane's heart to theirs.

At this point, we were beginning to see a larger picture of the gospel played out right in front of our very eyes: unwanted children were wanted by a loving father and mother. The father and mother were willing to go through extreme measures to adopt those children into their home because they WANTED them.

The kids didn't promise to be good, nor did they make any commitments to care for the parents when Mr. and Mrs. Lopez were old. Nope, it was nothing like that at all. Mr. and Mrs. Lopez loved the kids and rescued them so that they could be in a forever home because Shane and his sister were WANTED.

Wanted

I don't know that we have ever been able to tell this story without our eyes filling with tears. Shane, a messy little boy with more digits than normal, was wanted. He had a family who wanted him and his sister, and they wanted to make them both members of the Lopez family.

Danny Gokey, a Christian recording artist, absolutely nailed it when he wrote about how God wants us. I know that his song "Wanted" is about how God wants us, but I can't help but juxtapose those lyrics onto foster parents who show love for the fatherless among us. This is what we try to convince children of when they come into our home: we try to help them to see that they are wanted.

For our non-faith based readers I ask for a little room here, but that is the way God feels about all people who have ever lived. Rich, poor, black, white, young, old, smart, not-smart, plump, skinny, bearded, tatted, bald, big-boned—it doesn't matter who you are, God loves you and He wants you in His family.

And of course, God wants foster youth—every last one of them. The orphans all over the globe, He wants them in His family, and that also just happens to mean the one reading this book. Yes, you! God is crazy about you. He knows you. He knows everything about you. He knows what you have done—everything—and yet He loves you. He knows your story, your heartbreak and your pain; He was there when everything hit the fan, AND HE WANTS YOU! Yes, He saw what you did and what they did to you, AND HE STILL WANTS YOU.

That's what makes Christianity different from other religious systems. Most religious systems require that you perform so that you don't get punished. In other religions, the god(s) who is the object of worship wants you to fear them and to serve them and even make them happy so you don't suffer pain and consequence. In Christianity, God wants a relationship with you. God is standing ready to forgive you, to cleanse you, and to give you eternal life right now, this very moment. What's more than that, He desires to live in you so that your life is full of maximum benefit in the here and now. You are wanted!

That's the way the Lopez family felt about Shane and his sister: they wanted these two siblings! Sure, Shane's hands would require serious surgeries. Yes, there would be numerous specialists' visits in Los Angeles, which many times would require overnight stays. But that's a small price to pay when you love someone and you want them!

By now, Shane had been with us for 14 months—about 13 more than we were initially told—but at some point along the road, child protective services didn't want to move Shane until they knew for sure what the judge would decide. Was the judge going to award Shane and his sister to the grandmother or to the Lopez family?

The court trial was about a week long, and I have never been able to read that particular judge's facial expressions. The Judge eventually ruled in favor of the Lopez family. The grandmother's rights were terminated and the Lopez family was cleared to adopt the children. (Go ahead and wipe your eyes with that tissue, I will too.)

We cheered. We laughed. We wept. We rejoiced. But mostly we thanked the Lord. Shane was wanted by His Heavenly Father, and now he would have an earthly father who wanted him as well. God truly sets the solitary in families (Psalm 68:6).

I am so thankful that we were able to play a part in this providential undertaking of our Father. Shane and his sister would now have a forever home. They were adopted by Christ-followers, and Dawn and I were able to play a small part in this story. That's a win! That's a Super Bowl win! Send down the confetti—we're headed to Disney World, people!

At the time of this writing, I have just logged 31 years of service as a pastor. I have seen some amazing works of God in my "young" life. What God did with Shane and his sister—that was huge, maybe one of the most gratifying experiences of my life. Dawn would say the same without a doubt. We stood in the gap for a little guy during a time of his life when he couldn't care for himself, and now he has been adopted in a loving forever home! Mission accomplished. That is missional fostering: a temporary assignment; a tremendous cause; a timeless impact!

Oh, one more thing before I dismiss the class for the day. As an added bonus, Mr. and Mrs. Lopez have graciously allowed us to still see Shane! He remembers us and calls us "Uncle Jon and Auntie Dawn." (Wipe your eyes again now.) He has been out of our home for 1.5 years now, but the last time he saw Dawn, he grabbed her around her neck and said, "Can I keep you forever?"

I can see that Dawn wants the mic; I'll let her wrap this chapter up. After all, this is what she had visions of doing, so she gets to send us out today. This is last part of that Mother's Day 2020 journal post that I referenced earlier:

A Final Word from Dawn

I can't help thinking what if? What if we had not been willing to open our home to a kid who came from a really hard place? Where would he be? I believe God placed him in our home so that the entire course of his life could be changed. Now that little guy is going to hear about Jesus every day of his life. He is going to impact others . . . a ripple effect that I will personally never see the full implications of.

Class dismissed. Throw your tissues in the basket on your way out.

Discussion Questions

1. Is it possible that your heart could love someone who was not biologically related to you the way you would love your own flesh and blood? Give some examples.

2. How did you observe God's hand in this story?

3. For a moment, step into the mind of the maternal grandmother who lost her grandchildren. What emotions do you think she went through during the process of losing her grandchildren? Describe the roller coaster that the Lopez family must have gone through during their journey through fostering and the trial. How were Jon and Dawn's emotions different than Mr. and Mrs. Lopez?

4. How did the trajectory of Shane's life change from the moment he was removed from his unsafe living conditions? In what ways might his life be different now had he not been removed?

5. What conversations do you think the Lopez family had when they were thinking about adopting Shane and his sister?

CHAPTER 6

Amazing Grace

Here's where we are going: missional fostering involves a deeper understanding of grace.

There are times, many times when Dawn and I have felt like absolute failures in this fostering journey. Sometimes the mission is hard, and it requires on-the-job training so that we can play a greater role in more intensive mission work. Although we expected this training to come from educated professionals, God put us into "school" with an unlikely teacher. That is when He stretched the limits of our systematic theology of grace.

Tropical Storm Allie

Allow me to introduce you to a 10-year-old named Allie. Her parents' rights had been terminated, so her aunt stepped forward to adopt her. We have met this aunt and we found her to be a very nice lady. I don't know the reason Allie's aunt turned her back over to Child Welfare Services, but it is not hard to connect the dots.

Allie had control issues—serious control issues—and no one in this world wanted her around.

By the time Allie was placed with us, we had upped our game in the foster-care world. We had been asked to foster Intensive Services Foster Children. The title says it all, but maybe not enough. We had one ISFC teenager with us at the time, and Allie came to our home as a level 1 placement: the kind of placement that has "no issues, no real negative behaviors and no real problems to report". Level 1 placements are easy-peasy. Allie's diagnosis, however, was about to change.

Allie was jovial, jolly, and joyful when she walked into our home. She had serious "dad jokes"; I was impressed. I was convinced that I was going to have a long-term soulmate. It was the calm before the storm.

On her second day in our home, she went to school, but at 10 a.m. she told her teacher that she threw up in the bathroom. It was a lie; she just didn't want to be at school. She'd had such a good time with Dawn that she just decided to hijack the situation and go back to our home. Not cool.

On her third day, she went through our teenage ISFC daughter's things and stole $100. In the words of King James, "There was no small stir." "It" hit the fan, know what I mean? Loud expletives filled our home and all of our neighbors' homes as well. Normally one has to subscribe to Pay Per View to see a match the likes of what was going down in the foster bedroom. We, however, were able to watch for free. We rushed in to break things up and send them back to their corners.

At this point we realized that we had a ten-year-old with very elevated behavioral issues—higher issues than we had previously seen or experienced in our home. Allie was a level north of ISFC. Here's what we have come to understand: bad behaviors are the result of very deep wounds in the heart of an individual. That is what trauma does to a person; it injures them deep down in the secret places of their heart. Then, when they are triggered, they will react in such a way that they will often injure others in ways similar to the ways they have been hurt. Allie longed to control things in her life, so she was willing to steal, lie, and even harm people to get what she wanted.

The question I want to ask at this point in the chapter is, "What does a child like this need?" She has just rifled through someone else's stuff and she stole 100 large! She is only 3 days in our home for Pete's sake and we're dealing with petty theft!

Does she need to learn about consequences for her actions? Does she need to experience some tough love to help her understand what happens when you steal? Maybe she needs to know about the long-term potentiality that she might spend her life behind bars? That is where I was leaning. I was thinking that she was playing the role of the younger son of Luke 15, and I needed to help her. In my mind, Allie was the student with the problem and I was the teacher who was to help her learn some truth.

We were only three days in, so Dawn and I still felt like we had a good handle on the situation. But had they seen what was going on I'm pretty sure that oddsmakers in Vegas would have shifted their positions to favor the little one. Vegas would have been right; we were outmatched, unprepared, and oblivious to how deeply wounded and hurt a ten-year-old could be.

Allie's idea of coping was to try to take charge of the situation, to reach out and grab the wheel and steer the car for all she was worth. The question running through my mind was "What can we do to help this girl? It was obvious she had never learned about the pain of breaking rules, and as foster parents our hands were tied. But more than just limits and boundaries, Allie needed to know about our Great Healer, Jesus the Christ.

In hindsight, I can now see that I was wanting to teach her about the weightier matters of the law and boundaries and consequences, but God wanted her to learn about Him and His great grace.

Back to our story. King Solomon of Israel once quipped, "He who trusts in his own heart is a fool, but whoever walks wisely will be delivered" (Proverbs 28:26). Allie couldn't trust anyone but her own heart. After all, everyone in whom she had trusted in her ten years of life had abandoned her. Her parents had walked away and now her aunt had walked away.

How can you build attachment and trust when there is no one to lean on, to learn from, and to teach you these lessons? Foster parents play such a huge role in helping children to attach and begin the process of learning to trust in people—maybe for the first time.

Here's what Dawn wrote in her journal about that time: "*Trauma can cause otherwise beautiful children to do and say terrible things. Not all the time. Some of the time. These traumatized littles have beautiful, sweet moments, but I have also seen a terrified child act out in some extremely irrational behaviors. Extreme behaviors are the result of a lack of security, being bounced around, and poor decisions made by adults who are supposed to give love and protection.*"

By now, we were experienced enough to look past what Allie was doing; we had been taught to look past the behaviors to the hurt. That gave us compassion and sympathy. But what Allie really needed to learn was that there was a God in heaven who was crazy about her no matter how much she acted out. Allie could never out-bad God's grace. We are all on the naughty list, and that makes us all eligible for an incredible gift of grace.

Hurricane Allie

Give a tropical storm a couple of key accelerants and it can quickly escalate into a full-blown hurricane. That's what happened on our watch, in front of our very own eyes. If Allie did not like what was coming her way, it was like warm water to a Category 2 hurricane: Holy Toledo, Batman, you'd better batten down the hatches and board up the windows!

Allie's behaviors escalated while every relationship in her life deteriorated. In the words of a pop song, she came in "like a wrecking ball." She attacked her friends in her class when they got in her way. She destroyed her teacher's new iPad when the teacher put her into time out. She was sent to the office so many times that the school had to dispatch a special resource teacher whenever she was at school. Allie was churning out in the Gulf, about to make landfall. I'm so glad God doesn't allow us to know every detail of the future; had we known, we would have probably looked for an early termination plan.

In the 40-ish days that she was in our home, Allie finished the school day only four times. The principal, God bless that kind man, would later tell us that he kept her at school those four days just to give us a bit of a break. He understood the dynamics of traumatized foster children. Educators like this are making a difference in these children's lives.

On day 17, the eye of Hurricane Allie struck at her elementary school. Dawn was called to school because Allie was being "detained" in the principal's office. From the sound of things, the teachers were the ones being detained. Dawn walked into a front row seat of the disruptive forces that were being unleashed both in and from Allie. Eight adults were standing like a human shield around her so that she would stop destroying things.

She toppled tables; she poured milk on the computers in the lab; she would swing "crotch-level" at the men who stood in her way. She had been corralled in an open area outside of the office block of her school. The principal looked over at my wife with a gash over his eye. Allie was spinning out of control while everyone was waiting for the gale-force winds to die down.

At that moment, Allie had everyone's attention, but no one could get close enough to help. Social workers, behavioral wellness workers, teachers, counselors, WRAP-around services and SAFTY services (highly individualized and trained personnel to support youth with intensive behaviors)—everyone was in code-red mode trying to assist her, but when Allie was "flipped out" there was nothing to do but wait for her to wind down from the sheer exhaustion of it all. It was like watching the Weather Channel as they chart a Category 5 make landfall in the Florida panhandle and then it blows through southeast Alabama, finally dissipating over Tennessee somewhere.

Finally, Allie settled down. The worst of it was past, and all that was left now was to try to evaluate the damage so that everyone could assess their injuries. The principal apologized to Dawn profusely, but it was no longer safe for Allie to be around children. Allie was suspended. We totally understood because, who could blame him? The staff looked like Rocky Balboa after a bout with Apollo Creed! Somewhere deep down behind those big brown eyes there was a little girl who was in pain, and there were no coping mechanisms in her toolbox.

When Allie settled, she was then able to dialogue about what had happened with uncanny maturity and keen perception. She was always very sorry for the harm she had inflicted on her friends and those close to her. She was disappointed that she had hurt her classmates and teachers. She would in those cognitive moments acknowledge that she couldn't control every detail in her life. But acknowledging a truth and implementing a self-regulation plan are two totally different mental processes: Allie had no idea about how to do the latter.

Although I am not a licensed therapist, I am confident that this little one had been venting uncontrollably since she was a little girl. You don't just up and go ballistic as she did in a moment. Children get to this level of behavior because their needs have never been met. As a little child they cried, yelled, screamed, and banged their heads on the floor, but no one ever came. Do that enough times and you begin to lose confidence in all caregivers of any type. In time, you come to believe that there is no one who can care for you or your needs except for you! Allie vented violently in school that day because she had probably been venting violently all the way all along. I am confident that is why every caregiver had walked away from her.

What Does She Need?

That is the real question everyone was trying to solve. Her therapist assigned more counseling sessions. Her mental health clinicians prescribed stronger medications. Her social worker organized more individual mentoring services to teach her the proper coping mechanisms.

All of those were vital and necessary, but what Allie also needed to learn was a lesson from her heavenly Father. God wanted her to learn that no matter how far she would go, He would love her and pursue her. She couldn't do anything too bad for Him to be scared away from her. God's love is scandalous in its scope. No one is disqualified because of past performance; if God could save Saul of Tarsus (Acts 9), then by all means Allie could be offered grace as well.

The biggest problem to this lesson from God is that Allie's foster parents were not on the same page with God. Yikes! I still felt that Allie needed to learn and understand boundaries. Of course, we were sympathetic to all she had been through in life, but we thought Allie needed to hear a good dosage of the law. Looking back, I am 100% sure God was wanting her (and us) to learn about His extravagant grace. Who better to help her than a pastor? But unfortunately for Allie, the pastor/foster parent had some learning yet to do himself.

Life was hard for Allie. Did I mention that she also had leukemia when she was five? She had been in remission, but Allie still proudly showed us the port where they would give her the chemo. The amount of pain that this little girl had experienced in her short lifetime is more than many of us will endure in a hundred lifetimes.

After the school incident we treated her with "kid gloves," afraid that we would accidentally do something to set her off. Everyone agreed that Allie needed to be in a more intensive lockdown facility, but those are hard to come by, so we were asked to keep her in our home. A social worker actually said to us, "All you need to do is to keep her happy." Easier said than done. Meanwhile Allie's incident information and application was sent out to STRTP homes (Short Term Residential Treatment Programs) all over the state. STRTP homes are like group homes on steroids. We all waited for someone to accept her.

Allie was now running our home; we were just occupying the rooms and paying the mortgage. It was true that we were sleeping in the master bedroom, but that was all that we were the master of. I have been around some control freaks, worked for one once, but now we were living with one.

Everything had to go her way because we were fearful that another Category 5 could pop up out of nowhere. Allie's new role in our home meant that she now handled meal planning, portion size, and our social calendar. For the few days Allie was with us in our home, our lives were being directed with the threat of "if you don't do what I want, I will walk out into the middle of the street." We didn't believe her, so we called her bluff. She wasn't bluffing.

Big picture. Zoom up to 30,000 feet and look down on the scene. What did Allie need? Why did God leave her in our home for 40-plus days? Meanwhile there were mistakes being made by her social worker that delayed her removal from our home. Here's what we know: God kept her with us, in our home, under our care for a reason! There was something that both Allie and us needed to learn.

So God, in His sovereignty, concocted a plan: a crazy plan that He knew would work. Some of God's plans down the years have been quite crazy to human minds, but nonetheless effective. Ever heard of Gideon and his 300-man marching band? Or how about the kid with 5 pieces of bread and two small fish? God can even cause a virgin girl to have a baby—the Christ child! Nothing is impossible with God (Luke 1:37).

A lesson on grace? No problem. I understood grace for sure! I went to a Christian school, a Christian college, and I had been a pastor for almost 30 years. I have taught entire series on Grace, but not the grace that God was wanting to show. God's grace is extravagant. Scandalous. Relentless. God apparently had enrolled Dawn and I in a 40-day crash course, and I think the angels forgot to notify us of His plans.

The new truth that God had in mind for us and for Allie would change the way we saw life forever. Who would have thought that our missional fostering life would automatically enroll us in some continuing education units with the Divine Instructor regarding His amazing grace?

Grace 101.

Grace is God's precious gift to us when He gives us kindness and love at the moment when we deserve punishment! Grace is from God, and He is rich in grace (Ephesians 1:7).

Grace is getting a gift that you don't deserve. Grace is deserving nothing and receiving something nice, really nice. Grace proves that justification is by faith not works, can I get a *woot woot*! Paul, in his book to the church at Rome put it this way: "Now to him who works, the wages are not counted as grace but as debt. But to him who does not work but believes on Him who justifies the ungodly, his faith is accounted for righteousness" (Romans 4:4-5). That is grace!

Grace has never been about your performance or lack thereof. (Read that again, will ya?) Actually, grace is given to people who DON'T DESERVE IT. That's what happens when a person gets saved: they are given grace (a good and kind gift from God) because of their faith, not their performance. Paul put it this way, "For by grace are you saved through faith" (Ephesians 2:8). God wanted Allie, Jon, and Dawn to know that His grace was beyond their imagination. It was greater than Everest, deeper than the Pacific rim, and wider than the gulf between Republicans and Democrats in an election year.

Here's a teaser for you—how was God going to get past my systematic theological persuasions so that He could get His truth into the lesson plans? That was light work for Him.

One of the most challenging mindset shifts we have had with fosters is in those moments when we reward them when they do not deserve it. Don't judge me for being honest; I sense your self-righteous eyebrow beginning to raise. Hold your horses, and listen to the way this sounds: A child loses his mind and throws a royal fit. Then, instead of giving them what they deserve, you give them kindness, love, favor, and good things.

Whaaaaat? No way, Jose! That goes against everything that you think is right or appropriate. I know that words like "counterintuitive" and "countercultural" are trendy words to drop on your connect group, but when you actually have to use them in real life, that is much more sobering.

Here's what makes sense: When someone does wrong, talk to them about consequences, punishments, and throw out words like three strikes and you're out. The idea of giving grace to a child who is behaving badly is counterintuitive (I feel so trendy writing that). Why in the world would you give this child anything other than swift punishment? After all, we say to ourselves, "This child will repeat these behaviors if we don't crack the whip and make them sorry they behaved that way!"

Here's a newsflash: Our Father doesn't think like you . . . or me.

When God gives us something good at a time when we deserve something bad, that is grace my brotha! The apostle Paul wrote to the church at Rome, "Or do you despise the riches of His goodness, forbearance, and longsuffering, not knowing that the goodness of God leads you to repentance?" (Romans 2:4). Giving grace when someone doesn't deserve it sounds a lot like the good news gospel of grace.

God is good to people who don't deserve it, because that goodness will lead them to a change of mind about who God is. That was the point of the story in Luke 15 where the younger son ran away from the Father, then came back into a relationship with the Father because the son remembered how good and kind the Father was. His Father was so kind to the servants that the son was willing to settle for an employee-boss relationship just so he could get some food (Luke 15:17-19). The son came home and found grace, and a party, and a new robe, and a ring, and some new shoes, and a new relationship with his dad.

God is the author and founder of grace. God builds grace in one of the warehouses in heaven. God owns the patent and God is the supplier of all grace, and He is able to make all of that grace abound toward us (2 Corinthians 9:8). God gives us grace, not justice! Justice is what Christ experienced for us in our place (Galatians 3:13). Grace is what God gives to us because of the payment Christ made in our place. Grace is beautiful and it will take your breath away. Grace is the kindness and love of Jesus to us in spite of what we have done.

My moral compass was wrong. Way wrong. God used Allie to re-calibrate my theology of grace by teaching me about giving good gifts to "un-good" people. I was about to learn about grace from God's eyes.

Category 5 Hurricane

Here's the scene: a birthday party for a ten-year-old girl. Allie was invited. Cupcakes were involved. All seemed well when we dropped her off, but we were called to come back to the house and pick her up right away. I walk in the house in time to see Allie power lift a printer over her head and then slam it on the ground. I wondered if we should pay for their printer? This could get expensive.

Allie then fled the scene of the crime and went and hid under the bed in her friend's room. What set her off? Allie wanted two cupcakes, but there were only enough for everyone to have one cupcake. Allie did not get her way, and without any warning signs a Category 5 hurricane made landfall in Orcutt, California.

Unfortunately, the birthday party was no longer happy! Kids were crying—everyone just wanted Allie to go back home, and fast. I knelt down beside the bed and told her we should go home, but she didn't want to leave. Her friend's dad was with me and he kindly told Allie that maybe at a later time she could come back, but it was time for her to leave for the day. Allie refused, locking her arms around the bed post.

That's when God whispered into my ear. It was not audible, but it was definitely divine. "Jon, offer to give her something she doesn't deserve. Offer to take her to get some Krispy Kreme doughnuts."

I'm sure I bristled. Instantly the left side of my brain (the logical side) objected: "OBJECTION, GOD—SHE DOESN'T DESERVE IT. SHE HAS SINNED THE SIN, AND SHALL FACE THE PENALTY." Mr. Law chimed in his agreement with a verse or two about punishment and death. I felt bad correcting God, but apparently He must have forgotten about this thing called punishment. Good thing I was here to help straighten Him out, right?

I agreed with Left Brain and with Mr. Law. She certainly did not deserve a doughnut. That's when I felt like God told me again, "Give her grace; go get her a Krispy Kreme doughnut." As I reflect back, it sounds a lot like Peter's vision of the sheet from heaven in Acts 10.

Reluctantly, my mouth said words that I did not plan to say or even want to say; the words just came out in spite of me! "Hey, let's go to Krispy Kreme and get a maple-glazed doughnut." Allie stared at me like I was crazy in the head! She sat up, let go of the bedpost, composed herself and looked me in the eyeballs and with absolute sincerity she said, "Wait, I don't deserve it. Why would you do that?"

That's when God said through my mouth what I have never been able to shake. Again, God spoke to me and through me. "Correct. You don't deserve maple doughnuts, but that's what grace does for us. God gives grace to people who don't deserve it."

That's what makes grace so attractive. It is based on the merits of Jesus, not us. A righteous God gives grace to us because of the performance of His perfect Son, Jesus. Grace is given in spite of our works. Savor the aroma of that last sentence. Having preached thousands of sermons over the past couple of decades, I have had times when words were put in my mouth at the moment they were needed, but none that impacted me like those words did. Allie stood up, gathered her things and walked out of the house like nothing had ever happened. With a smile and a wave of her hand she said, "Goodbye everyone," and she hurried to the car.

Yes, we did go to Krispy Kreme. I bought the doughnut, but only one doughnut! I was still trying to process how my "bribery" could have been anything like grace. And how could I just turn my back on everything she had done and give her something so rewarding as a maple doughnut? God had some 'splainin' to do! He wasn't done with me yet, or Allie for that matter.

I wish I could tell you that episode awakened Allie to what she was doing, but instead it seemed to embolden her to jump into the driver's seat of her life. The end of her time with us was near, but she had one more gust in her, and I had one more test from the Father to see if I was tracking with Him about this session on grace.

It hit critical mass a few days later. Allie lost it when she thought we bought something for our other foster daughter. In Allie's mind, we were being unfair. We had bought nothing; Allie was absolutely mistaken.

Allie charged into the foster girls' bedroom and began to destroy everything that her foster sister had. Drawers were emptied. A new iPhone was hurled against the window. Everything on the walls was pulled down as she went charging through our home like a bull in a china shop. Allie had lost it again. She was throwing more punches than Muhammed Ali in "The Thrilla in Manila." We called our social worker and anyone else who would listen.

Dawn and I were exhausted. Our plan was to get her out of the house with a social worker, then lock the door behind her and never open the door again. It wasn't our finest moment. I am not proud of how tired, exhausted, and irritated we had become.

It was then that God whispered the words of grace into my heart again. "Give her something she doesn't deserve. Buy her something! Give her some money and let her control how she wants to use it!" I bristled again. I'm pretty sure a little bit of bile came into my mouth to be honest. "Give her something when she doesn't deserve it? Who does that, God?" He didn't answer, but if He would have, He would have said that He is the One who gives bad people things that they don't deserve!

The idea was from God. I take no credit; God was using my mouth and my wallet to do things that I had never thought about doing. I held out a $5.00 bill and told her that I wanted her to go to the dollar store and get something. She sat up, looked me in the eyes and replied in a similar fashion as the last time, "Why, Jon? I don't deserve it." Again, words came out of my mouth from Christ in me. "You are correct, you do not deserve it, but that's what grace does. It gives us what we don't deserve." Grace is the most beautiful thing in this world.

Those were the last words I was able to say to her: words of grace about a God who gives us good things when we don't deserve it. My very last words to her were about a God who gives grace to undeserving people. How perfect. How filled with the hope of the gospel. God kept her with us long enough for us to tell her about Him and His scandalous grace and his reckless love!

Still Working It Out

Just reminiscing about our brief time with Allie brings me angst. My understanding of grace was shallow, my view of God was not accurate, and I am thankful for the child that God used to reveal this truth to me. I wish I had understood our gracious God sooner. I didn't know God's grace. Not deeply. Not really. Not the way God was teaching it to me now.

I think Peter, one of Jesus' disciples, nailed it when he said, "But grow in grace" (2 Peter 3:18). Grace is something we grow into. We have grown in grace because of our journey into missional foster care. We are not experts in grace; we are still doing the homework problems God has assigned to us. There is nothing like grace. No wonder John Newton called it "Amazing."

A disclaimer. Without any doubt, our time with Allie was our most difficult time of fostering, but it also happens to be our most rewarding. Not all foster care is as intensive. This story is not normal, and we have discussed the possibility that something like the Allie story might discourage some of you from getting involved. It is our prayer that you will hear our deep gratitude for how our lives have been changed for good through shepherding children from hard places.

Discussion Questions

1. Unpack this statement found early on in the chapter. "Bad behaviors are the result of very deep wounds in the heart." What is the connection between our reactions (or retaliations) and the condition of our heart?

2. When Allie faked sickness so she could go home, what was she looking for? Put yourself in her shoes for a moment and think about the deep issues and needs she would have had due to her leukemia, the abandonment of her parents, and then of her aunt.

3. Compare and contrast bribery and grace. How are they similar? How are they different? Consider Romans 4:4, Ephesians 2:8, and Galatians 2:21.

4. How was your understanding of grace impacted in Jon and Dawn's interaction with Allie? How does grace encourage you?

5. How could grace change families that are full of bitterness and hurt? How could grace allow a mate to forgive their partner who cheated on them? Why is grace so important for foster-care parents?

CHAPTER 7

Runaways, Fosters, and CSEC

Missional fostering puts you in the toughest trenches with the incredible medicine of the gospel.

Ok, kids, this chapter is not for the faint of heart. This chapter will get raw and real. If you are reading this with your children, discretion is advised.

Story 1: "Hi Dawn, I'm Running Away"

Living his life on the run from CWS, sleeping under a bridge, and stealing from the convenience store so he wouldn't starve was Julian's life. He was a worldly-wise young man living in the body of a very lean 14-year-old. His build was slim, like he hadn't a good "comfort-food" meal in a couple of years. Probably Julian's most outstanding characteristic was his skater vibe, which included baggy skater pants, a tie-dye shirt and very long hair which flowed from under his flat-bill hat.

I don't remember the exact reason that he was moved to our home, but one of the things that he told us about was that the parents in the foster home he had just run away from wouldn't let him wear his hat in the house. Dawn and I made an executive decision: the hat would not be an issue for us! His hat rarely left his head.

As foster parents, we aren't allowed to ask questions about a foster's past, but if they bring up the topic or if they ask questions or for our advice, then we are certainly allowed to "prudently parent" them. Julian's only request was that we keep him enrolled in his karate class. Of course, we wanted something of continuity to stay in place in his life, so we drove him to karate class—a 30-minute drive one way! During those long car rides Julian would feel safe enough to open up and little bits of info about his past would seep out. At one point, he told us he had suffered sexual abuse from a relative in his past. Sad and disgusting, but true.

Sometimes when kids begin to open up and tell you their story it just breaks your heart. Sometimes it makes you cry, and sometimes it just makes you feel dirty when you hear the details of what they have been through. To be honest, it is hard to get some of those stories out of your mind. Julian's mom allowed her male friends to sexually exploit him, so when Julian was old enough to know what was going on, he ran from the only parent he had. That's when he found out that he could survive on his own by hiding under bridges and overpasses.

Although I was never totally sure of the veracity all of the stories he would tell, there were some things that you just knew down deep had really happened. I suspected that Julian had been in a gang and maybe pimped out before he ever came to our home. Research reveals that when foster youth bolt, pimps have an uncanny ability to find them. Exploitation and trafficking are the way of life for those kids when they are found by a pimp.

When a person gets hungry enough, they will do anything for food. Anything. Esau sold his inheritance for some chili. Runaways will trade their innocence and their bodies for food if they get hungry enough.

For the first month when a youth comes off of the streets and is placed in your home, there is a "honeymoon period." They try to fly under the radar, stay within the lines, and get some traction. If they have been on the run, they are often exhausted and physically in poor health.

When they feel safe, protected at night, and have full tummies, they begin to relax. Family life is exciting. They get to go to the doctor and the dentist immediately. They usually get a clothing allowance upon arrival in a foster home, so they can be suited out with all of the essentials to get them ready for life and school.

Julian had an amazing honeymoon period with us. We watched his karate matches, and he would eat wings and sit through college basketball games with us. He loved frozen yogurt, and each time we went to the Froyo shop, he would fill his cup to capacity before setting it on the scale to weigh it. As I watched him load his cup, I will admit that I thought about giving him some weight limit parameters, but I never did. He was in a happy place in his life, and it felt so good to give him good things.

Although Julian had a very unpleasant memory of his mom, he always treated Dawn with respect. I don't think she had to open a single door anytime he was around because he would rush to where she was and open the door for her. I love honeymoon periods with the kids! Like all good things except for Jesus, they do not last forever.

We should have known trouble was brewing after the CFT (Child and Family Team) meeting. This is a mandatory meeting for all foster children so that the foster parents can get a handle on how things are going at school. Julian never had homework because apparently he was always "able to get it all done at school." We didn't buy it, but the most important thing in his life was not his grades.

In that meeting Julian's house of cards came down around him. His teachers exposed his lies and his truancy to us. We weren't mad, nor were his teachers. Everyone was glad he was holding his stuff together. The meeting traveled through the typical circle of conversation: "We are disappointed; you can do better; let's work together on this; you can do it! The sky is the limit with you!" Our experience with educators is that they are eager to help foster kids succeed, and without exception they go the extra mile to help them to get through. It is our guess that Julian felt like doom and gloom would await him when he got home because we found out about his lies. Maybe he was embarrassed, but we don't know for sure.

Dawn left the meeting and told Julian she would be back to get him after school. As Dawn was sitting in the car line her cell phone rang. It was a number she did not recognize. She let it go to voicemail. Out of curiosity, she listened to the message.

She has it saved on her phone, and we play it periodically to remind us of how real the struggles are for these kids. Here is the transcript: "Uh . . . Hi Dawn . . . It's me, Julian. I'm running away. You're gonna have to call Drew [Julian's social worker]. I don't know what to say, but yeah, bye."

That was it, he was gone. On the road again—but not what Willie Nelson had in mind, I'm sure.

"Karen"

Dawn dialed the number back but there was no answer. She tried again, and finally when a young man answered, Dawn went all MOMMA BEAR on him. She was convinced that this kid was hiding Julian—she just knew it. She told him if he knew what was good for him, he had better tell her right now where Julian was hiding or there would be Sheol to pay! Few things in life compare to a foster momma who feels like she needs to go into protection mode! Hell hath no fury like . . . a foster momma who is separated from her cubs.

She threatened to call the police. Then she threatened to march into the school office and give the number to the principal so that they could find out who this young man was that was aiding and abetting a runaway! She was speaking this kid's language, and he broke under her interrogation. Her 16 years of being a youth pastor's wife had come in handy, and there are many former teens that we have to thank for this! She was the "bad cop," and there was no "good cop" to come to this kid's aid!

Actually, come to find out, the kid on the other end of the line was an innocent freshman who had let Julian borrow his phone to make a call. The boy was just being a good neighbor; he didn't even know Julian—he had never seen him before. He was just sitting there on the wall when Julian rolled up on his skateboard and asked to borrow his cell phone to call his mom. Now, according to officer "Karen," he was going to the slammer, and kids like him didn't survive well in there. His life was over! (Ok, ok, I'm kidding of course . . . kinda, sorta.)

Julian was gone; running is a part of his defense mechanism. It is how he protects himself from further trauma. It is a coping mechanism for sure, but not a good one, because when he gets uncomfortable or when he feels he might get rejected, he bolts. It is not hard to run this problem fast forward and see the significant issues that lie ahead for this young man if there is no change.

We called the sheriff's office and filed a report. Everyone was on the lookout for a skater dude, but it was no use. Habitual "runners" have an M.O. that makes them very elusive. Although the boys in blue were all on the lookout, Julian knew what he was doing—this was not his first rodeo.

A couple of hours later, one of Julian's karate instructors spotted him walking down the highway leading from town. He thought that was odd, so he called us. Officer "Karen" went out to look, and even called his social worker (a.k.a. the foster-kid magnet because he has this uncanny ability to find foster kids when they run). It was no use; Julian was gone. He would surface about a week later about 15 miles down Route 1 in Lompoc, California, a small city on the coast.

One of Julian's teachers who lives in Lompoc saw a skater dude whisk by on his board. He had baggy skater pants, a tie-dye shirt and a straight-bill hat. She knew who it was instantly. Curiously, he was carrying a briefcase while riding his skateboard. His teacher was able to catch up with him. Julian was nice enough, but he told her that he needed to roll, because he was "making a delivery." Her imagination went wild and her heart sank. This wasn't Domino's or Door Dash; this delivery had something to do with the briefcase in his hand.

She called us and we told her to call 911. She did, and with all the stealth she had seen in thriller movies, she followed from a distance as Julian rode into a hotel parking lot and went in unit #10. She staked out the joint until the police arrived, and after hearing her story, they knocked on the door and searched the unit. You guessed it: Julian was long gone. At the time of this writing we have no idea where he is. He is still on the run; he has been so for maybe 6 or 7 months.

When any child runs away it is tragic, but the parents and close family friends often get out in cars and drive the neighborhoods looking for the troubled child. When foster youth run away, the search and rescue team is a lot different, and many times the results are different as well. Bio children get mad and they run, but they usually come to their senses and head back home. Foster youth get mad and run, but they do not always have the same magnet inside their hearts to draw them back home.

Story 2: A Picture, a Trash Can and a Memory

Recently, I was divvying up chores with our two foster girls. I said to the youngest that she needed to empty the bathroom trash-can. The older one had to clean everything else in the bathroom. Simple, right? Doing chores around the home was nothing new, but it certainly was different that morning. She immediately went into a fit of rage.

Here's a piece of background information that absolutely played into the story. A few days earlier, that twelve-year-old girl had been told by her social worker that there was no chance of a reunification with her mother in her case plan. There is no way she was going to ever go back to live with her mom. The girl said ok, and went off to run and play and have an amazing visit with her social worker, whom she really adores. That was on a Friday. Saturday, Sunday, and Monday were normal days for us. We thought that everything was good.

Unbeknownst to us, below the surface, she was volcano waiting to erupt. Fast forward 4 days, it is now Tuesday. The trash-can chore conversation happens. She snipped, "I didn't put any trash in it, why should I take it out?" Now, that was clever of her. Parents who don't foster teens miss out on some funny moments!

Sometimes questions don't deserve answers, and sometimes no matter what answer one gives, it will not be the right one. Every parent knows what I'm talking about, right? I smiled, although only with my face not my heart, and then gently replied, "Because we all share in the chores; that's what families do" (understood "duh" at the end of my explanation).

She had lived in a group home since she was four. Her dad was not in her life, and her mom's rights had been terminated. She had just experienced her first Thanksgiving and Christmas in an actual home with an actual family. She had been with us for all of five months, and that was the longest she had been in a home with a family since she was old enough to remember.

She is truly a sweet girl, but something snapped inside of her. The term clinicians use is "triggered." In the mental health world, "trigger" is a word used to describe the reason for a current emotional state of extreme distress. Triggers can be a sound, an odor, a specific phrase, or even just a memory. Taking the trash out wasn't the real issue; it was the trigger that reminded her of a previous issue—the real issue.

One of the best things you can do in those moments is to try to de-escalate the situation with peaceful tones, kind words and a concerted effort to divert the child's attention to something playful and fun. Mental health professionals would never quote James the apostle when he wrote that "the wrath of man does not produce the righteousness of God" (James 1:20), but they would certainly agree with the truth in that statement. When an individual gets mad and flips out, God's righteous work is not being done. Really nothing good comes when a person begins to lose control, and she was like a rocket during the countdown timer, waiting for the launch! Three, two, one . . .

Because she is a quiet person, we had no idea of what was going on inside of her. She was like a duck, paddling 90 miles an hour under the surface, calm and peaceful above the surface. We had not engaged her with her coping measures over the last 4 days because we had no idea she was churning on the inside.

She stood up and she began to stomp out of the room, taking the trash can out to the dumpster on the side of the house. From there, she got on her bike and hit the streets. Dawn was tuned in to what was going on, so she watched our twelve-year-old ride all the way down the street. Sometimes kids need a little space so that they can process issues on their own terms that they can control. Foster children often feel like they can't control anything in their lives, so doing things on their own terms gives them some sense of power and strength. Going for a ride was one of her coping mechanisms. She was riding her bike—this was a good thing, right?

Our young one had never ridden her bike outside of the neighborhood before, but after Dawn didn't see her on our street, she got in our SUV and she began patrolling the streets of our neighborhood. It was now late afternoon, and the sun would be setting in about an hour. After several laps around the neighborhood, we called the Santa Barbara County sheriff's office, because she had not come home, and we worried that she wouldn't know how to get back home. You can never tell how much kids know about directions when they are riding in the back seat of your car, know what I mean?

Our SBSO boys in blue are AMAZING. An officer showed up within moments, took down her info, and even snapped a photo (of a photo) to send out to the other officers on duty. Surely it wouldn't be hard to find a twelve-year-old on a blue cruiser bike who just happened to be barefoot, right?

Because foster youth runaways are so vulnerable to abduction and exploitation, everyone goes into code red when they take off. Our first call always goes to our social worker, a young man in his early 30's named Drew. Drew is like a Major League Baseball catcher—he can catch just about any kid who ever runs away. He thinks like they think, and I have often teased him that he is probably the same mental age as the kids. We have worked with Drew for several years and he can always find the kids who allude the police. Drew jumped in his car and began to look at the usual spots that fosters go to when they need to cool off.

Fast-forward an hour or two now. It was almost dark, and Dawn's phone rang. It was our SBSO officer reporting that they were putting a chopper up in the air to help look for her! I LOVE THAT! They didn't want her to be out in the dark and they were fearful that she might be lost and not know how to get home. Big props to the cops! Operation Find the Twelve-Year-Old Foster Girl was now in high gear!

Our young one had been gone for a couple of hours. Everyone was on the lookout, even the eyes in the sky hovering around in the heli. When the helicopter is circling above your neighborhood and you actually know why they're up there, you feel like a Boss!

We set up a control center in our home—well, not really, but the adrenaline really kicks in during those moments. Dawn and I broke into hostage recovery mode just like the teams that you have seen on TV. We were ready for the ransom call, and we weren't going to negotiate with any scumbag who would take her. (Admittedly, we should probably tone down our Netflix binge watching)

Who does she know? Have her friends heard from her? What about her mom? What is her social media account saying right now? Can we trace her phone . . . Oh wait, she doesn't have a phone yet!

This runaway story happened to end well, not like Julian's. Drew, the foster-kid magnet, found her riding on a sidewalk a couple of miles from our home. By that time, she was cool, calm, and collected. She agreed to get into his car and come home. We notified the SBSO, and the search party was called off. Our child who was lost had been found. The fatted calf was prepared and we made merry with our family. There was music but no dancing (our kids tell me I don't have good dance moves anymore, even in celebration! What do they know! But I digress.)

When runaways come home, they usually don't want to talk about what just happened. No way, no how. She bounces back into the house like nothing has happened, nothing to see here, keep moving along people, "What's for dinner? I'm starved!"

Truth is, they are too vulnerable at that time for any poking or prodding around for dialogue. Whatever you get at that point is fake news. We played along like nothing had ever happened. We figured she would talk when she was ready.

Many times we will never know what triggers a youth to run because many times our kids have not come back. In the case of this little one, she began to drop some clues in the hours after her return. She wanted us to know what was going on, but she wasn't going to use her words or complete sentences with logical explanations—no, that would be too easy! So she began to drop clues, but we were going to have to follow the popcorn trail she was putting down.

Clue # 1 came when we were eating dinner. I stood from my chair to help myself to a well-deserved second portion. After all, the last couple of hours of life we were running in turbo mode. That certainly equates into a faster metabolism, therefore, any additional portions were probably going to burn up as soon as they went into my mouth (that's my story, and I'm sticking to it.)

When I arrived back at my seat, an old picture of our foster girl and her mom was on my chair. No explanations, no conversations, just a picture. Oddly enough, no one saw her put it there. That was the only clue that she would give us that night; something about the picture was the key to unlocking the reason why she ran. We entered it into evidence as Exhibit A, but she quickly took the picture back and refused to dialogue.

Resource teams met with our young 'un the next day but they got nothing. Dawn and I even broke out our most highly trained surgical methods for extraction of information—the skills that we had honed working with teenagers in the youth group for 16 years. We got nothing either. It was like talking to the Sphynx! As waterboarding is not a viable option in our state, the only thing we had to go on was just that photo.

We knew her reason for running away was bigger than the trash can; we knew it had something to do with the picture, but we had no real idea how it all worked together. A few days later she was talking to one of our friends at church and she said, "I ran away this week because I saw a picture of me and my mom when we were little and it made me sad that I can't live with my mom." Bingo! There it is, that was Ground Zero. And that, my friends, was the trigger!

A simple old picture triggered a memory, and the memory triggered an action on a bike to who-knows-where. By God's grace, she was found by her social worker. This story, though not a fairy tale, does end with a "happily ever after" ending for her. Not all foster youth are as fortunate.

In a May 2014 article about preventing and responding to foster-care runaways, the NC Division of Social Services noted that 66% of runaway youth returned in two weeks or less. According to research performed by Pergamit and Ernst (2011), girls are more likely to run away than boys.[1] "Runaways tend to have more school problems, higher rates of suicidal ideation, more reported behavioral problems and more alcohol, substance abuse, and mental health disorders. The more placements they have, the more likely youth are to run."

---

1 practicenotes.org/v17n3/runaway.him

According to research performed by Natasha Latzman and Deborah Gibbs:[2]

1. 19% of youth who were placed in foster care after the age of 10 ran away from foster care at least once.
2. 17% of those children had an allegation of human trafficking while on runaway status.
3. Of the 70% of youth with a human trafficking allegation during runaway status, the first identified victimization occurred during a foster-care runaway episode.

Someone once said that "prostitution is the youngest business in the world." The. Youngest. Business. Let that statement sink in for a minute.

Commercial Sexual Endangerment of Children (CSEC)

CSEC is an acronym for Commercial Sexual Exploitation of Children, and unfortunately it has become serious business in our world and even in our own country. CSEC is big business, and bad business, particularly for foster youth. CSEC is a 32-billion-dollar-a-year industry.[3]

CSEC can refer to the publication or posting of child pornography and would encompass everything from photos, videos, books, and even audios of sex acts. With the advent of lightning-fast internet and live streaming from any wifi device, no child is safe. Runaways are incredibly vulnerable—particularly those who think (as many foster children do) that they are a fifth wheel and don't feel a strong pull toward home.

The connection between foster youths in the child welfare system and CSEC is staggering. A 2014 DOJ report estimated that 85% of girls involved in CSEC were previously in the Child Welfare Service.[4] In 2015 it was reported that 59% of all of the children caught

2 acf.hhs.gov
3 static1.squarespeace.com
4 Ibid.

up on prostitution charges were in the foster care system. Foster youth are increasingly vulnerable to human trafficking because they are more likely than their peers to have had experiences of exposure to domestic violence and issues of maltreatment.[5] According to the It's a Penalty Organization,[6] one in six runaways will be lured by a sex trafficker and forced into prostitution within 48 hours of being on their own.

Typically, youth are bribed into the commercialized sex trade industry by a handler who seems to take a real interest in them. Fosters crave connection and attention, so the handler will seek to build a strong, caring relationship. This individual is kind and generous and feigns that he or she is genuinely concerned about them and their story. That narrative will continue for a while, and then the gifts will begin. The children will be offered nice gifts: stilettos, MK bags, designer clothes, and premium skateboards. Handlers have deep pockets for their recruiting purposes.

Youth who are homeless and looking for some food and a warm bed for the evening make an easy mark. It starts with a relationship of trust, then it deteriorates quickly into a physical relationship, and by that time it is too late—the kids are trapped. They have no idea what they got themselves into, and they have even fewer ideas on how to get out.

In most cases when children are brought into the sex trade industry, they are beaten and raped many times so that they give up their will to fight or escape. Children often blame themselves and begin to think of themselves as "whores," so they are just getting what they deserve. This guilt is exacerbated when and if they find moments of stimulation or pleasure within the abuse. That's when their moral compass whirls around, never able to find true north. If it's so bad, why are they aroused? And if they are stimulated, that must makes them complicit with the action, right? You can see how confusing this must be to a young mind. When they begin to believe the narrative that the handler communicates to them, they stop fighting and become complicit with their new life.

---

5 acf.hhs.gov

6 itsapenalty.org

Runaway foster youth have nowhere to run back to. In many cases, no one is searching for them.

I am finishing this chapter shortly, yet I do not leave you with positive, pleasant, and pragmatic plans for how we can take down this Goliath of an industry. The problem is enormous, and awareness of its entire scope is still beyond the grasp of our information at this time. The fact is, this is a real pandemic, and one that does not seem to have any containment. CSEC is like a wildfire burning voraciously on the hills and ridges of California, fueled by the Santa Ana winds! We are not even thinking about words like "containment" at this point.

For every twelve-year-old who returns back home, there are dozens and dozens of kids like Julian who don't come back. Maybe a great way for us to land the plane in this chapter is with a quiet prayer for those innocent and vulnerable foster youth who are trapped. Stop your safe life for a moment and tune out the noise. Then, think deeply about the fate of those children and their lot in life. Every day they wake up to a horrible situation.

Every child who is trapped in this industry is someone's child: someone's little boy or someone's little girl. There is a grandparent out there who goes to bed every night wondering what happened to that precious little bundle of joy who used to bounce so playfully on their knee.

Finishing this chapter with some calls to action seems appropriate. Maybe it is time for you to get off the sidelines and suit up, because the game has already started, and our team is having to play some serious catch-up!

Pray for foster youth.

- Pray for their physical safety and protection.
- Pray for their emotional stability.
- Pray for their eyes to be opened to the Father who loves them.
- Pray for the demise of the sexual exploitation of children.
- Pray that the perpetrators of these crimes on children would be caught and that their seedy network would be exposed and dismantled.

Follow foster care causes.

- Google and follow foster care social media pages.
- Observe causes in which you can get involved that support foster youth.
- Find out how you can donate your time as a tutor.
- Find out what it would take for you to be a mentor to a troubled child.
- Be an adopted grandparent to a child and make sure they have what they need at Christmas and on their birthday.

Call up a foster agency or your local county foster care agency and schedule a sit-down meeting with a social worker.

- Find out how you can volunteer as a designated driver (not the one that you are thinking about—the one who drives kids to and from appointments)
- Find out more about how you can "babysit" some kids so that the foster parents can get a date night.
- Ask about short-term foster care.
- Ask about long-term foster care.
- Find out about fostering as a means to adopt.
- Fill a suitcase for a child: think of what a 10-year-old boy or girl would need on day one if they were brought into the system from an unsafe home situation.

Call up the local branch of CASA (Court Appointed Special Advocate) and ask about how you could be an advocate for a child.

(And this is not necessarily a political statement, but if the shoe fits . . .) Vote for politicians who are tough on sexual crimes against children.

Discussion Questions

1. When Julian's life of lies was exposed, he ran away. What underlying factors might have prompted this reaction (insert yourself into his story and try to see things from his perspective). What impact do you think it had on Julian when his mom let him be violated by her male friends?

2. Jon told a second story about the twelve-year-old girl who ran away a couple of days after she received some bad news. What does that teach us about Post Traumatic Stress Disorder?

3. Explain in your own words how the picture of the girl and her mom "triggered" her to run away.

4. How have your eyes been opened in this chapter to the sex-trafficking industry? What role do you think the porn industry has played in the endangerment of children?

5. Of the five calls to action at the end of the chapter, which one resonates with you the most and why?

CHAPTER 8

Don't Try to Be the Hero!

Missional foster parents don't have to be the hero; we just have to point those in our care to Him.

I love being the hero, the star, the MVP, the guy who steps up to bat in the bottom of the ninth with the bases loaded, and all eyes are on him to get it done. I can remember Michael Jordan saying in one of his interviews that when the game was on the line, he wanted the ball in his hands.

When I was in junior high I would go to the batting cages with my dad, and I would pretend that each pitch that came from the mechanical arm of the pitching machine was my chance to make the game-winning hit. I played hundreds and hundreds of scenarios in my mind that would send our team to victory because of my heroic at-bat. In my image-driven mind, it was epic! I could just see all of the fans cheering and even charging the field; the team rallying around me, hoisting me onto the shoulders of the seniors! Then, I would look over at the bleachers and all of the high-school girls would wave, and the next day walk up to me by my lockers and even give me their phone numbers. I never wanted that dream to end!

Who doesn't want to be the hero, know what I mean?

Believe it or not, that scenario actually happened (kinda/sorta) in my freshman year of high school. I was one of the youngest players chosen to play on the varsity baseball team. It was mid-April in Atlanta, Georgia, and to this day I could have sworn that there were major-league scouts in the stands. I walked up to the plate with the bases loaded, our team losing by one. There were two outs in the bottom of the seventh (FYI, high-school games only have seven innings), and the fate of the game was now on my shoulders.

I don't remember how everything happened, but when the pitch came, I swung for all that I was worth, and maybe a little more. I think the Lord sent an angel to direct the ball to hit my bat. It was a drive to deep center field over the heads of the outfielders. I think the ball might still be flying because I jacked it good! The tying run came across the plate, and then the go-ahead run scored! Game over—we won—I was the hero! It had happened like I had imagined! The team rushed the field, we jumped around in a great big huddle, but I didn't get hoisted to anyone's shoulders, and none of the high school girls were at the game that day. Other than that, my dream to be the hero came true.

Being the hero was fun, I'm not gonna lie. The coach actually was nice to me after the game. I didn't have to carry all of the equipment back to the locker room, and the seniors didn't give me a wedgie on the next road trip. For a brief day or two, at least in my mind, the world was a bit happier, and I walked a bit taller. Reality hit three days later when we played our next game. I think I struck out all three times I batted. The Lord did not send any more angels that year, and my days of being the hero were over. I was back to being Jon, the freshman who batted ninth in the order again. Easy come, easy go. I guess God was just preparing me to be a foster parent. Being a foster parent is not heroic, it is just normal, every day parenting stuff.

When a youth comes into our home, we look at them in the eyeballs and we pretty much rehearse the same speech verbatim. "Hey dude. We're glad you're here. We're going to have some amazing food and you will have a nice warm place to sleep. Usually Thursday night is wing night. We have this magic list that Dawn keeps in the pantry, and whatever food is written on that list will usually appear after she has shopped for groceries. We're glad you're here, dinner is around 6-ish, you're gonna love it, and we're already loving having you here."

Generic. Normal. Nothing spectacular. For sure nothing superhuman. Nothing even remotely supernatural. Nothing heroic at all. Nothing that requires being faster than a speeding bullet or more powerful than a locomotive. I guess that is a very roundabout way of saying that anyone can do what we do!

If I could describe fostering in just a simple sentence it would go something like this: Just be a parent for someone who needs one. No need to be a hero; certainly not a savior. You are not responsible to provide a happily-ever-after ending for anyone, because that is beyond your pay grade. Just focus on being a short-term, seasonal employee for our Father in the temporary role of caregiving. Leave the soul work to God, mostly He needs us just to help with the schoolwork.

Here's a thought I want to chase down with you. Heroes are not needed because the Hero already came! I love that.

Over my years I have heard so many people say to me, "Dude, I could never do what you do."

At first I was flattered, but over time I have begun to push back a bit. I now usually say something like, "Oh really? You can't cook a meal? No? Or share the empty bedroom in your home? You can't drive a kid to a football practice, or sit at a softball game cheering for a girl who is not biologically yours? Which part of that sounds too hard for you? Let me know what sounds heroic to you and I will make sure to wear my cape the next time you're around."

Because I say it with a smile I feel that I am well within the limits of speech that is full of grace and seasoned with a bit of salt! Our job as foster parents is really as simple as being a substitute parent for a short time to a child who is in need. And lest you forget the mission, we want to point them to the Hero every chance we get.

Because the Hero came, all He needs is humans. Just be a parent, because their parents are having a tough time getting their stuff together right now.

The Savior Complex

One of the cautions that we try to talk about with people who are thinking about foster care is the "Savior Complex." It could be true with all parents, but it especially seems to resonate deeply within the faith-based community. Our church tribes find deep meaning in life as we follow the Savior, and even try to mimic Him. This always leads us to disappointment, but we usually give it a try until we have to stop over the sheer exhaustion of the effort.

Yes, Jesus rescued us from destruction and now lives in us! This gives our life meaning, purpose, and direction. As we are inspired by His example, many go into being foster-care parents. So far, so good! But some have a glamorous idea that they will get to be the Rescuer of the needy children in their charge. Just because Jesus is our Hero, don't think you can sign up for foster care and save fatherless kids!

I must confess, I like the missional sound of rescuing children, but that kind of talk needs a bit of tempering. If God burdens your heart to serve fatherless children, then you need to recognize what your role is, and that role is very simple: Be a prudent parent! Leave the saving to Jesus!

Foster parents are not the star of the movie; often we are not even one of the leading actors. We do not get a special dressing room with our name on the door, nor does anyone ask foster parents to come in early and get a little make-up before a placement comes to our home. Missional foster parents are simply substitute parents.

There is a Savior who can heal every child, and He is alive and well today. If Jesus were living today, He would be the One who would be hounded by TMZ and the paparazzi. Well, what is our part in this drama, you ask? We are the unnamed individuals in the crowd providing background faces and filler noise as Jesus walks on to the set. In the words of LaVar Ball (if you do not appreciate the NFL or the NBA, then this name will be wasted on you) in his now infamously disrespectful retort to a female reporter, "Stay in yo lane!"

The Hero of the Story?

The Hebrew Scriptures are filled with amazing stories of bravery, courage and victory. Every time I read the story about Benaiah I think to myself, "I hope that Dawn doesn't actually read this story and expect something like that from me!" Dude, Benaiah should be in all serious conversations of the G.O.A.T.S Hebrew history! I should have named my first child Benaiah! You remember him, right? Benaiah was one of David's mighty men who chased after a lion (who does that?). The lion jumps down into a pit, and Benaiah jumps in after him! (No, I am not kidding! Read 1 Chronicles 11:22). To make things more epic, he does so on a snowy day! He kills the lion and then crawls out of the pit victorious and lives to tell about it. Benaiah is a picture of Christ, the Hero of the Bible. Jesus is the One who chases our adversary, the devil, the one who stalks about as a roaring lion (1 Peter 5:8)! Jesus is the One who came to the earth, killed the lion, and came out of the pit on the third day victorious! Benaiah is a picture of Jesus, not you!

Here's the good news: you don't have to be anything like Benaiah to do missional fostering. You don't have to have Iron Man-like powers before you can volunteer or foster missionally, or even adopt. Just be you.

While it is certainly true that we can play a small part in changing the trajectories of children's lives, there is no room for anyone else in the lane of the One true Hero. And I hate to burst your bubble, but when kids come into your home, you need to remember that they are bringing at least one traumatic event, maybe many traumas with them. As a result, very rarely do you see anything positive in the short-term. Foster work is vital and necessary, but usually we only begin to see positive impacts in the lives of children in the long term.

Jesus is the One the fosters need to see. Technically, we are not allowed to push or coerce any child in any way toward religion of any kind. But here's what I have noticed: if Jesus is living in you, the fosters will see Him soon enough. And believe me when I tell you, they will ask about Jesus soon enough! When they hear us pray to Him and identify ourselves with Him in our everyday lives, they will ask about Him!

Claire

Claire was beautiful and brilliant. By far, she is the smartest and most articulate of all of our placements. She graduated from high school at the age of 16: for the record, that was faster than any of our biological children! Here's a fun fact, she would even watch Shark Tank with me. This girl was legitimately brilliant! She is the only foster child that asked if I would extend her wifi hours so she could do her homework. She was a rock star.

Although my memory of all of the details is a bit sketchy, I do remember that Claire had been abandoned by her mom, and then adopted by an older couple (we will call them the Smiths). As fate would have it, the Smiths went through marital problems, and Mr. Smith eventually left the home. Mrs. Smith was left to raise this adopted child alone. Big props to her! Being a single parent is hard.

By the time Claire was a teenager, Mrs. Smith was showing signs of early onset dementia. She was often cruel to Claire, so at the age of 16, Claire turned herself in to Child Welfare Services. CWS brought her into our home. Claire felt unwanted, and who could blame her? I believe that was part of what was driving her to excel at everything. I believe Claire felt that she had to prove that she was worthy and valuable by outperforming all of her peers and associates. But feeling the need to prove yourself all the time is like a hamster getting on one of their wheels.

Unfortunately, Claire was strongly opposed to God while she was in our home, and still is to this day. We have a healthy and warm relationship, even though she has never acknowledged a need for God in her life. If you ask me, I would say that our impact on her life has been minimal to this point and certainly not that of a savior! I am thankful it is not up to me to do soul work on the kids.

Here's another layer to the Claire Mission. Even though kids aren't always ready to get on the Jesus Train while they are in our home, sometimes our relationship with them allows them to reach back out at a later date just to talk or to get advice. That's what made the phone call in October 2020 from Claire a cherished memory.

Although Claire was a rock star according to CWS standards, she was still deeply wounded by the rejection that she felt from her mom and then Mrs. Smith. That is a heavy load for anyone to carry, especially a foster child. In Claire's mind, there were only three people she had left in this world that really cared about her: one of those three was a long-time friend, and the other two were, you guessed it, Dawn and me. A very small circle indeed.

Somehow in the course of life, Claire felt that her friend was trying to terminate their longtime friendship. That's when my phone rang. I'll go ahead and call that a win! Anytime a foster child reaches back out to us after they are gone, that is a God thing!

She was at critical mass. We didn't talk about Shark Tank, or school, or her new vegan diet. Rather, the call quickly became a time for me to listen to her as she ranted about how her only friend had treated her. Claire is quite the wordsmith, and there were certainly some words I think she could have used a little less frequently! (Actually a lot of words since we're on the topic.)

Claire just needed to talk to someone who would listen to her without judging her. So, what was my role? Listener. Not very superhuman at all if you ask me. She needed an ear and I happened to have one free that night. She gusted and howled and finally wound herself down about 45 minutes into the call, and then she said those words I was hoping to hear. "What do you think?" Music to my ears! Now I had a chance to speak into her life!

It was then I assured her that there was a God who loved her and knew what it was like to be alone and rejected. Jesus alone could understand what she was really going through. Only the Hero could heal her heart and bind her wounds. I didn't say much—she has heard it before. She listened quietly, then quietly offered, "I expected no less from you." We talked superficially for a few more moments, but a listening ear had been what it took to get her away from the edge of the roof. I mostly listened. That's what fostering is. Just being a parent to a child in a time when they need someone. They use us as needed, and they move along. Not heroic at all.

There you go, that's as close as it gets to playing the hero. Wise people know who the true Hero is. Pointing someone to the Hero and then getting out of the way is one of the best things we can do for anyone, including a fatherless child. That's missional fostering: keeping our eyes on the Hero and helping those in our care to see Him. Having assets and resources may enable you to help care for kids with style and a little bit of bling, but your bank account is not the answer, the Savior is. Besides, the kids will at some point spill Coke all over your nice SUV.

The Hero Lived, Died and Rose from the Dead

If you are not a Christ follower, I want to thank you for getting this far. For a pastor, I think I have done a fairly good job of not cramming religion into every paragraph. For 30 years, people have paid me to talk about Jesus, and yet I have tried to allow this content just to flow. Try not talking about the most important thing in your life for about 9 chapters and see how you do! That's like asking LeBron to make conversation with you without bringing up basketball! Good luck with that.

I suppose you could skip to the next chapter, and I won't judge you. In fact, I will never know.

There is one more thing about the Hero that I want to highlight before we move on.

In the third chapter of Genesis, God made the first "shadowy" promise of what the Hero would do when He came. There was a crisis: the only two people on the entire earth disobeyed and essentially led a revolt against God. God did not kill them, but the sting of death had been successful. Adam and Eve and everyone after them would die because of Adam's choice. Sin, destruction, abuse, neglect, violence—it all began in that moment when Adam and Eve sinned. The picture was bleak. But God did what He always does: He pursues us and He makes a way for us to be right with Him again. God provided hope for humanity with the promise of a Savior who would come (Genesis 3:15).

It was then in that garden that God began to tell us about the Hero. He started to give us little pieces of information that would help us to identify Him when He came on to the scene. The Hero would be born from the family of Abraham, in Bethlehem, of the tribe of Judah. He would be preceded in life by a forerunner, and somehow He would be born of a virgin and would travel to Egypt. He would teach in parables, would begin his ministry in Galilee, and would perform miracles by healing people who were blind and lame. The Hero would ride into Jerusalem on a donkey and experience betrayal by a friend who'd been given 30 pieces of silver. He would be forsaken by those closest to Him. He would die by a crucifixion, His clothes would be gambled for, and He would be offered sour wine at the time of His death.

Thousands of years came and went. Little by little the books of Jewish history began to paint the picture of how this Hero would be different than all the other men who had ever lived.

The sheer volume of prophecies that this Hero fulfilled is astounding, but how could He be a real Hero if He died? The only way that Jesus could be a real Hero would be if He could save us through his sacrificial death and then somehow come back to life! That would make Him different than any and every other leader of any faith system. Interestingly, that was exactly what the prophecies said about Him. The Hero would conquer death and rise again on the third day. Impossible, right?

Only one Man has ever been able to fulfill these specific prophecies, and his name is Jesus the Christ. Jesus is the Hero. That is what makes Jesus different from any imam, preacher, pastor, teacher, prophet, priest, or king. Jesus was not just a good guy: Jesus predicted his own death and resurrection! And it happened just as He said! *Boomshakalaka*!

Who does that? A true Hero does! I am so thankful that all that is needed from foster parents is just to show up and point their kids to the Hero through their words and deeds.

The Hero Came to Heal the Brokenhearted

This will probably sound like an infomercial: "BUT WAIT, THERE'S MORE!" Not only did Jesus the Hero come and die on the cross for our sins and then rise from the dead on the third day—Dr. Luke the physician in A.D. 65-ish recorded this story regarding the life of Jesus. It is found in Luke's gospel, chapter 4 verse 18:

> "The Spirit of the LORD is upon Me,
> Because He has anointed Me
> To preach the gospel to the poor;
> He has sent Me to heal the brokenhearted . . ."

GOOD NEWS: The same Hero who fulfilled the specific prophecies above and dozens more just like them is the same Hero who promised that he had the ability to HEAL HEARTS!

Who can heal people? A true Hero, that's who!

Jesus claimed that He could cure hearts that were broken. Jesus didn't practice on people; He healed them. (Read that again.) Jesus didn't experiment on people; He cured them.

I am grateful for the professionals who work in the mental health field. The doctors, psychiatrists, and psychologists who practice and prescribe medicine play a vital role in the life of foster children. Yet in all of my dealings with mental health professionals, I have never heard any of them promise to be able to heal anyone. They don't even pretend to try.

- Treat them? Yes.
- Practice on them? Absolutely.
- Prescribe meds to help to regulate unhealthy behaviors? Without a doubt.
- Cure anyone? Nope.

Only a true Hero can do that! That's why the Hero came, to heal those who had their hearts broken. That's His specialty!

That's what makes the role of foster parents—and particularly missional-minded parents who are in it to positively impact as many lives as possible—so important. The Hero is the Healer and He lives inside of all of His children. I am not the Hero, but since the Hero lives inside of me, I just need to let the fosters come close enough so that they can get infected by Him. "Christ lives in me" (Galatians 2:20). "Christ in you, the hope of glory" (Colossians 3:11).

Every foster child has their own heartbreak; in fact, each one probably has several of them. For Claire, it was the thought of being rejected yet again. Here's the good news, the really good news: the Hero came, and while He was on earth, He promised to have the cure for every heartache and heartbreak. His cure is better than a vaccine, an immunization or even an injection. His cure is a relationship!

That's why we don't need to get into fostering to be a savior for some poor child: because we don't have the cure; only Jesus does. Jesus is the cure! If you knew that you didn't need to be some sort of superhuman, just a normal human, would you be more open to getting involved?

Lean into what God awakens inside of you. I read a mural on a wall the other day that said "If you are looking for a sign, maybe this is the sign that you have been looking for. So do it."

Just sayin'.

Discussion Questions

1. Have you ever thought that foster parents were somehow different and specially endowed by God to do the work they do? If so, why did you think that?

2. Jon refers to Jesus as the Hero often in this chapter. How does this hit you? What did Jesus do while on earth that would authenticate Jon calling him the "Hero of the world"?

3. What are some ways in which you have tried to be the hero of a situation or a cause? What was your experience? What did you learn?

4. A few paragraphs above, Jon talked about some of the specific prophecies that Jesus fulfilled. How does that help to authenticate Jesus in a pluralistic world where there are many "ways" to eternal life?

5. How does Jesus heal people? Look up these references and talk about what changes in us at the time of the new birth: Jeremiah 24:7, 1 Corinthians 2:16, 2 Corinthians 5:17, 2 Peter 1:4, Colossians 1:27.

CHAPTER 9

Redefining Wins and Losses

As I am writing, I will often stop and pray that God will use this book to encourage members of the faith-based community to enlist in the mission of fostering. Maybe you adopt, maybe you don't, but I do pray you will join the ranks in some form or fashion and care for the neediest among us. If God answers this prayer of mine and you enlist, then I want you to be able to stay in the game for the long term. This will absolutely and necessarily involve recalibrating your mindset.

I'm not gonna lie, we have seen some big wins in our time in missional foster care.

God's Forgiveness

Angelo came to us as a runaway who had been found in a different county about 100 miles to our south. If memory serves, he had been on the run for a couple of months, and he was sick. Because he couldn't get better, he walked into our county sheriff's office and turned himself in. He knew that by doing so he would get to see the doctor and get some much-needed meds.

Angelo was one of those kids that I connected with instantly. Our lives couldn't have been more different: his dad was in prison; my dad was a pastor. According to him, his mom worked the street corners; my mom worked in children's church. He had grown up in the school of hard knocks; for the most part, I had grown up in the paths of instruction that my parents had taught. We were polar opposites, but my heart was connected to him from the very start.

Angelo was the youth that first introduced us to the power of the "magic brownies"—know what I mean by magic? One of the surefire ways you know that your young 'un has had a magic brownie is when their behavior is 180 degrees opposite of the way it was before they went to school. They can deny it all they want, but you know and they know that you know. But getting them to admit it is only half of the battle. The bigger challenge is getting them to give up the person who sold it to them.

Our city has seven junior high schools, and each one has a cartel running the school. Ask around, and you'll find that it's sad but true.

It took a day or two, but Angelo finally confessed to eating the brownie. However, no amount of persuasion could get him to give me the name of the kid who sold it to him. Being an idealist, I believed that if we could just get him to give up the members of the druggie gang in the school, the kids would get expelled and the principal would be able to protect Angelo for doing the right thing. I was really proud of Angelo because he went to the principal's office and identified the group that was providing the school with the drugs. The principal assured us that he would handle things discreetly and that no one would know it was Angelo who informed him.

Yeah, about that. I don't fault the school officials, I think they are incredibly devoted educators, but somehow, something didn't go as planned, and Angelo was identified as the guy who "ratted" on the drug suppliers. He denied it, but as their suspensions were served and the pre-teen cartel members came back to school, Angelo was "jumped" in the bathroom.

Once again I made my way to the principal's office to negotiate a safe educational environment. Everyone wanted the same thing, but the only solution was "protective custody" in the school. Angelo was removed from all of his classes and placed in the school resource office. That did protect him during class, but the real danger times were lunch and the breaks between classes. Angelo was constantly looking over his shoulder and second-guessing whether or not he should have cooperated with the school officials.

One night at about 10:30 pm I heard a knock at our bedroom door. I heard Angelo's voice, "Jon, are you awake?" I was silent, not making a sound because it was 10:30 pm, and everyone knows that's the time of night when you want to go to sleep, not answer questions about whether or not you're awake! But the knocking continued, a bit louder this time. "Jon, can you help me? I need to get God's forgiveness for some things."

Those words sent me out of the bed like a missile out of a launching pad. I feared the worst, thinking that maybe he had somehow found another brownie. "Of course, I can help with that—I happen to know God loves you very much and He delights in forgiveness and reconciliation."

For the record, Dawn and I are not permitted to push or promote our faith upon those in our care. That would be unfair coercion. However, if kids who have been in our home want to discuss matters of politics or religion and they bring the topic up, we are permitted to be true to our core values and beliefs. Jesus nailed it when he said, "Let your light so shine before men, that they may see your good works and glorify your Father in heaven" (Matthew 5:16).

That night Angelo confessed to God that he was a sinner. I had never told him that he was a sinner; his own conscience had witnessed against him. I had never heard of someone so young being a party to some of the things I heard in that prayer time. I love that our God specializes in the mercy business! That night Angelo bowed his head and opened his heart to a Savior who loves him, wants him, and is able and willing to forgive him of every sin that he had ever committed in the past, or will ever commit in the future. That is the type of win that I was praying I would get the chance to see when we got into fostering.

I would love to tell you that life settled down for Angelo after he was saved, but it didn't. His principal recommended that we try another school where he could get a fresh start. The petition to change schools was granted and although there were no more brownies,

Angelo struggled to fit into his new school. Sometimes the safer schools have more snooty kids.

It just so happens that Dawn and I were celebrating our 25th anniversary with a bucket-list trip to Italy about that time. Angelo was happy for us, but he kept asking us when we came back if he was coming back to our home. We assured him that he would; we wanted him there with us. We were able to find a home for him while we were gone, and I even arranged for us to have daily Skype calls.

I don't understand all of what happened, but a couple of days into our Italy trip we were informed that he left the home and was on the run again. Our hearts were saddened.

To make a long story short, he was caught in an act that facilitated his need to visit the juvenile detention center for a little bit. He remembered Dawn's cell number, so for his weekly phone call he called her and asked if I would come and visit him at the detention center. We went into a glass cell that was observed by a guard. It was there Angelo gave me a run-down of what he did that merited his stint in juvie. He wept with sorrow over the things he had done. I felt like I was sitting in a confessional. Once again I was able to remind Him of the God who loves him and has forgiven him of all of his sins. These words have encouraged millions down through the years: "For I will be merciful to their unrighteousness, and their sins and their lawless deeds I will remember no more" (Hebrews 8:12).

We have not heard from Angelo since, but I am so grateful that He has a companion with him, in him, who has forgiven him and is helping him wherever he is at this moment. That's a win: a big win!

Over our years of being foster parents, three foster teens have trusted Christ Jesus as their Savior while they were stationed in our home. All praise to God and the work of His Holy Spirit to draw them unto Himself. Those are some wins that will pay dividends in the next life. That is what happens sometime in missional foster care: sometimes people see Jesus in your life; they ask questions about how they can have what you have, and they begin a relationship with Him. I would like to tell you that has happened with every child, but it hasn't.

Wins like those take years, even decades. In all three of those cases, people had been seeding the soil of these young people's hearts for years. If you need to see quick results and souls getting saved then you will quit your post, throw in the towel and walk off the court before halftime. Fostering is a marathon, not a sprint.

I needed to have a paradigm shift in my thinking for us to enjoy the normal rhythms of fostering. Here's what we did: we made some calculated and strategic adjustments to our thinking. It has made a huge difference with us, and I am convinced it will be a help to you as well.

Redefine a Win!

For the first 16 years of my career/ministry, I walked the sidelines coaching teenagers. If there was a game, we were there to win! I would pride myself with my coaching record, although I would cover my pride with a false humility that sounded something like this: "Well, we are just trying to do our best out there. The boys really worked hard" (a.k.a. please notice the coach who prepped, trained and coached up those boys to do what just happened on that court!).

There are two problems with making wins about who has the most points: 100% of the time someone is going to lose the game, and 50% of the time it could be your team. Playing a team and losing by 50 points is demoralizing, no matter how many times you say it is about building character! No one will ever believe you. Am I right or am I right? So wins and losses must be about something more than the score.

Early on in my coaching career I redefined winning. A win had two components: a good testimony and hustle. If we kept a good testimony that reflected Jesus during the rigors of the competition, and if we out-hustled the other team, that was a win! It became my mission statement for all of our teams—Testimony and Hustle. We even put it on shirts and uniforms "Testimony + Hustle = Everything."

When we were able to make wins about character and not points, we were able to scale the program by leaps and bounds. In the end, our records were overwhelmingly successful, but the focus was on a new definition of wins and losses.

So, what is a win for foster youth? Let's break a win down to a small, measurable action that can be quantified and qualified:

Wins are life skills that we teach, model, and hopefully impart. Some are caught, some are taught. Without question, shifting your fostering mindset to life skills is crucial for you to enjoy the missional fostering of children for the long haul.

Wins of Foster Care

Fostering kids is like watching grass grow or paint dry—you don't see much of anything good happening in the here and now. What you do see happening is usually discouraging: truancy in school, a lack of concern about homework, and a general disinterest in life. If you make success about a child's grades in school, well, I fear you won't last long as a foster parent

Fights, skipping classes, and failing grades are the norms for most teens in the system. Many times they are unengaged in your family life, non attentive during corrective conversations, and lifeless when it comes to just about everything except their social media feeds of course.

I am 100% sure that there must be some teens who get placed into loving homes that immediately begin to succeed, soaring to new heights of achievement. There may be kids out there like that, but it is more likely that you will be placed with a child who has no interest in school whatsoever! Even if the children coming into your home are younger, they will almost always be developmentally, socially, or even physically delayed in some way. They will be riding in the wake of their peers in class and may even be labeled as a child with "special needs."

You can't define yourself by your apparent success with foster children, or even your own children for that matter! Your identity must be rooted in Christ, and your service must originate in that place of strength so that you can exist in a world with foster youth who are seriously lagging in just about every area of life.

So, let's redefine wins and losses. Let's not set the bar at "all passing grades" or "no trouble in school." Let's set a bar with these kids that is more realistic. No, I don't mean that we dumb down life for them; I'm talking about setting a bar that recognizes their history, their baggage, their trauma, and their destiny in adulthood.

This is what I'm thinking: they woke up with their own alarm? Win! You are now 1-0 my friend! They made it a day at school without a fight? Win! (Let's make it 2-0 my man!) They didn't visit the principal today? Win! (*Woohoo!*) They did their laundry by themselves? Win! They stayed away from the magic brownies? Dude, let's celebrate!

Let's make wins about teaching life skills that are necessary to live like an adult without the aid of government programs. Fosters, particularly teens, need to learn the skills of life that are necessary for them to become a good citizen and a functioning adult.

Here's another little tidbit: Dawn and I have tried to encourage ourselves when we *teach* them life skills, not necessarily when they *do* the life skills. Learning these skills is crucial to their development, and they are things that we can teach that don't require us an Ivy League educational background. This is where the rubber meets the road. This is bottom-shelf foster parenting. These are the new wins.

Teaching Nutrition

Talk to any teen about eating healthy and their eyes roll, but to many foster teens a soda and a bag of chips is a well-balanced meal. All kids would probably argue that those are two of the basic food groups, but some foster kids have had to survive on snacks, sodas, and fast food because mom and dad were not around and unhealthy food was. Healthy food is expensive, and fast-food menus have dollar-menu items, so many foster children (particularly teens) will come into the system in an unhealthy condition.

Any home-cooked meal they eat may be the first one they have had in a while. Our fosters love family dinner. We don't go all keto on them, but we do have home-cooked, healthy food, and the kids love to walk in the kitchen and just stand around and watch Dawn prepare. It helps that Bobby Flay has nothing on her. To be honest, I don't know if our own bio children fully value healthy food, but we continue to dialogue about it and model it. While they are in our home they eat healthy—win! They pack a healthy snack—win!

Hygiene

Do you remember how long it took you to get your junior high son to wear deodorant? And he grew up with you, right? Multiply that challenge by 10, and then prepare yourself to ask every day, "Did you put on deodorant? Did you brush your teeth? Did you flush? Did you use toilet paper? Did you wash your hands?"

One of the realities of foster care is that a host of teens were never taught proper hygiene from their parents as a child. No one helped them to learn to clean themselves after elimination and many times they were never taught how to brush their teeth. Newsflash: That is why they're in foster care, right? We have seen some quick wins when it comes to simple things like win.

Money Management

The longer a child has been in the system the more broken their thinking is when it comes to money. If a youth has been in a group home, they understand that "the system" provides everything for them: clothes, makeup, shoes, glasses, allowances, transportation, and a mostly consequence-free life! If the child breaks something, they have never had to pay for it: "the system" just replaces it for them. If they punch a hole in the wall, someone will come in on Monday and fix it.

We win when we can show and tell them the value of money. Because foster youth have been given so many things, they have never had to save for valuable items, and consequently they simply aren't capable of understanding or appreciating the value of goods. When they get their allowance, their idea is to go to the candy store and spend it all on Skittles and Airheads! (Don't send any hate mail, I didn't know that your grandma made Skittles at the factory until she retired. I have nothing against either of those fine products, but wouldn't you agree that they are not financial investments that hold their value?)

You win when you help them set up a bank account. You win when you encourage them to save for big items and require them to help replace the items that they destroy. These are all small wins. We even try to help them learn how to make money as entrepreneurs. One of our foster girls now looks for things that are free that she can turn around and sell to make some extra money—that is a win. She is on her way to being an entrepreneur and maybe she will get her day on Shark Tank!

Relationships

We model proper relationships. Most—dare I say all—foster youth have not received appropriate parental love, therefore they have no concept of how to love. (Read those two sentences again, would you?) Unfortunately, their concept of love and relationships is learned from media and movies. Ugh. The girls in our home have little concept of how to show appropriate love to men. They are vulnerable and susceptible to any guy who shows any interest in them. All teens, but especially fosters in particular, confuse lust for love. It is a win for foster youth to do life with a family where the mom and dad love each other and their children in an appropriate and safe way. That is a relationship win!

Helping foster youth to know what is healthy and unhealthy in the area of social media is crucial. I'm not saying we are winning in this area, but I'm telling you that missional foster parents can play a huge role in laying some foundations that the kids may or may not have received from their biological parents. One of our house rules when it comes to phones, tablets and all electronic devices is that we get the passwords, and we reserve the right as prudent parents to check any device when we feel like we should. Sometimes we even write up a contract of behavioral expectations and some ground rules for the phone. Prudent parenting requires us to turn the wifi off on their devices at bedtime so that they can sleep. These are wins because they are life lessons that any wise parent would teach their child.

We once had a foster girl who was identified as vulnerable to CSEC. She put highly filtered pictures of herself as her profile photos on Snapchat and her other social media accounts. She had hundreds of guy friends who would tell her she was beautiful. They would tell her how much they loved her, that they wanted to marry her. Some of them were in countries in Central Asia. They promised to bring her to their country when she turned 18 so that they could marry her. Then it happened—without exception, without fail, the guy would ask for a nude photo!

Another of our foster girls (who was twelve at the time) came home from a visit with her mom and the first words out of her mouth sent a chill up my spine. "My mom said I can get pregnant, but she wants me to wait until I'm 18." I had a hard time not saying, "Your mom is an idiot!" Instead of saying anything bad about her mom, I just tried to talk about how great it is to have a happy marriage with my best friend who has showed me her commitment by marrying me.

You say, "Dude, I don't see the win." The win with relationships is in the modeling! Relationship lessons are some of the ones that are better caught than taught. The win is in getting to talk about how wonderful it was that Dawn and I waited until we were mature and married before we had kids. You might ask, "How do you know that she listened?" I don't. I can only hope that she will watch the relationship that Dawn and I have, and that she will want what we have. Remember, the win is in the teaching of the lesson to kids who might not otherwise have heard the instruction.

Use Your Words, Not Your Fists.

I know, I know, I sound like a soccer mom sitting at a coffee shop telling her 3-year-old to stop banging the table with the spoon: "Use your words, Sawyer."

It is easier, and even safer (for fosters and maybe even your bios) to throw items, break valuables, and harm people than it is to dialogue with fitly chosen words. Think about it: If you really told people how you felt about them, would you still have any friends? Fosters don't use their words because some simply have no words to express how they feel. Some have used their words, and it backfired on them, and their social worker was given a 14-day notice to remove the child. Nevertheless, the life skill must be taught: "Express your feelings with words." That is a life skill that will help them for sure, right?

Fosters already feel like they are about as valuable as an old newspaper and as messy as a soiled diaper. They say to themselves, "That's why no one has adopted me: I'm so messed up! What good does it do to use my words? That can only make things worse, right?"

One of the best ways to encourage using words is by not reacting when they finally do get some unsavory words to come out of their mouths. Cool, calm, and collected reactions from foster parents will without any question lay a foundation for better and more effective communication through words.

Home Skills

Skills around the home are probably some of the most important to teach, yet are consistently the most lacking with fosters. That is why they are in your home, right? They don't know how to care for things or to pick up after themselves. As a general rule, they don't know how to do laundry. Teach a foster to make their bed—win. Teach them how to put away their toys—win. Teach them to hang up their jacket—win.

One of the things that I have admired about Dawn is the way she teaches both the girls and the guys how to shop for groceries and to prepare meals. I take fosters with me when I go to the gas station and have allowed them to perform the credit-card transactions at the pump. We work in the yard together pulling weeds and pruning our veggies. We talk about careers and jobs that they might enjoy. We teach them how to use the city transit system so they can get around from place to place. We talk to them about wage-earning vocations and even use all of the social workers' connections to help them to get part-time jobs. These are little wins that will help you to stay on-mission when the work seems long and unfruitful.

Preparing foster youth to "adult" means teaching life skills that really anyone can teach. As foster parents, these skills become ours to teach. Teaching life skills, that is a win. Count it. Keep score. Take the win. Tell everyone your coaching record, and re-calibrate your thinking on wins and losses.

Speaking of losses, as I look back at this chapter, it seems that I have not taken time to mention the losses. So, before it gets too late, I wanted to mention a couple of thoughts on the losses of foster care.

The Losses?

Huh. Yeah, I guess it is fair that we talk about the losses as well. Well, let's see. Give me a second to look back through my notes. Still looking. Be patient with me. Still looking. Huh. It seems that Dawn and I have re-defined losses as well. We can't think of any losses with fostering. How do we lose when we are sharing love? Do we ever lose when we invest in people's lives? As we love our neighbor (which certainly includes the fosters and orphans among us) as ourselves, we're simply doing what Jesus commanded us to do. That's mission. That's missional fostering.

So, no losses—it's all wins, baby!

See how cool it is to re-define wins and losses?

Discussion Questions

1. What are "wins / expectations" that parents often have for their own biological children? Why is it unfair to juxtapose these same expectations on foster youth in your home?

2. Jon mentioned a couple of necessary life skills in this chapter. Discuss how each of them play an important place in the role of a youth who needs to learn to live as an adult in this world.

3. Why do you think it is so easy for a foster youth to get tripped up with vices like the "magic brownies?" Were you surprised that Angelo found them at his junior high school?

4. Over the years, Jon and Dawn have had three children give their lives to Jesus in their home. What ingredients could you attribute to these "wins?" Who are some of the other players that help to play a part in successes?

5. In chapter 4 Jon mentioned some of the things that he and Dawn have gone through while fostering. Why do you think he says that there are no losses, just wins?

6. How could re-defining some expectations help to give you some wins with your family and friends?

CHAPTER 10

Myth-Busting: Missional Fostering and Recalibrated Thinking

I feel like we should all hum, "Who ya gonna call? Ghostbusters!" to help set the mood for what comes next. (Ok, I'll do my part and you do the humming . . . go ahead . . . I'll wait on you! A little louder if you don't mind.)

Although we are not especially long in the foster care life ourselves, when we became aware of the great need that surrounds foster children, it became our mission to talk to everyone about it. We don't receive referrals, and I really can't think of a time when we have received any kind of a kickback when someone joined the ranks of the few . . . the proud . . . Fosters!

However, I want to go after elephants in the room. You probably already know the elephants I'm talking about, the many reasons / myths that people give for why they can't get involved in fostering work. Are you housing an elephant in your family room? It sits there making noises and destroying furniture, but you simply refuse to acknowledge its presence.

The elephant is wearing a sandwich sign that says, "I'm not fostering because I heard ______________." What is your reason? What myth is circulating through your cognitive thought life?

I have come to believe that many people are looking for reasons why they should NOT foster. Maybe you have heard one of these, maybe it has bounced around your mind since we began this hike together. I really don't think fostering is right for everyone, but I do believe every one of us can get involved in some way.

So, as I get out my bazooka and take sight at these myths, I want you to think of Jesus in the temple overturning the moneychangers! Here we go.

Myths Debunked

Myth # 1:
I will get so attached that I won't be able to let go when they leave.

Yes, absolutely! That's the goal! *Ding ding ding* . . . we have a WINNER! That's how you know you are doing it right. Our friend Laura Weiting, who is also a foster mom, makes t-shirts that say, "I get too attached." Hopefully you WILL get so attached that it will break your heart when they leave. What you declare to be the problem is actually the solution to the problem . . . look at you!

Here's what missional foster care looks like in a sentence: They come, you do your job, you fall for them, they don't know what to make of you, they leave, and sometimes it breaks your heart when they leave. Mission Accomplished!

The job of foster parents is to fill to the brim the heart of that little one with all of the love they can possibly handle. There is a real possibility—and an even greater probability—that they don't understand what love looks like. Since we really have no idea how long they will be staying with us, our mission is to love intensively. Daylight is burning. Get going because they will probably not be with you forever.

Maybe by now you can see the problem with this myth. I don't mean to be rude (well, maybe a little), but I hope that I am not discourteous. The capital letters that follow are there for maximum effect, and actually I am meaning to YELL AT YOU!

FOSTERING IS NOT ABOUT YOU. OR YOUR ATTACHMENT. OR YOUR ACHY BREAKY HEART! (Shout out to Billy Ray Cyrus not necessary.)

Fostering children has nothing to do with your attachment, it's ALL about theirs: Are they able to attach to adults at all? Can they receive love? Do they even know what love looks like, or will they grow up, impregnate (or be impregnated), and repeat the fail again?

Making foster care about how much you might get hurt is an extremely self-centered concept. What about how they have been hurt: their victimization; their neglect; their trauma. That's the point of missional fostering.

We don't foster so that we can love without getting hurt. No one goes into relationships that way. We foster so we can give love, and yes, attachment! That's the name of the game.

Is it possible your heart is going to get attached? Absolutely. Is it possible the kid's heart will attach to yours? It's possible but not as likely. The child in your care is there because of an attachment fail on the part of the bio parent. Most fosters have attachment issues. They don't know how to "latch on," and that is why it is crucial for a mature and loving foster parent to come alongside of them and attach to the child so that the child can have a glimpse of what normal relationship attachments look like.

We have cried when some of the kids have left. Early on in our journey, we had a little guy named David placed in our house. He was about 2 years old, and he came to us with a man-bun on his head! Up to that point, I had never been a proponent of man-buns, but this little kid rocked it! Adorable—so much so that I have seriously considered one myself.

He was with us a couple of months, and they were filled with giggles and Latino dance moves the likes of which we had never seen before. This kid was a heartbreaker in the making. Then he was reunited with his maternal grandmother and a reunification plan with his parents began. Our hearts were broken. We cried when he left.

But the system won! The Little Guy won! The bio parents were given a pathway to reunification and that is a win! We won because we were a part of the process. And our attached hearts were broken into tiny little pieces, but our hearts healed because Jesus came to heal the brokenhearted—remember that part?

When Shane left after having been in our home for 14 months, our hearts were again smashed! They moved him on our wedding anniversary—what a downer. We were attached, and we still are attached, and we talk of him often. At the time of this writing, Shane has been with his new family for a year and a half, and we just got invited to dinner at their house tomorrow night! We are giddy with excitement! Are we attached? Heck yeah, even to this day!

There have only been a few times when our hearts weren't attached. In full transparency, those were times when the child was not with us long enough or the attachment process was so brutal that we felt like we had been in a fight with a chainsaw.

So, why would we subject our hearts to that? (You know the answer to this by now, don't you?) Because it was never about our hearts in the first place, right? It was about a fatherless child who was coming out of a hard place —and God's express command to love our neighbors.

Your heart will recover. You will comfort your heart by looking at your iCloud photo bank, and you will find yourself eagerly awaiting the next placement so you can start the process all over again.

Myth # 2:
It will mess up our family dynamic.

There are times when the mojo is so good in families, that families can become (wait for it, this is a new term) biological idolators! I'm not sure I made that term up or if I read it somewhere, but I am 100% convinced it's a thing. (Again, I am waiting on Webster. He really needs to get a copy of this book.) Although it is not officially a thing with a definition in Daniel Webster's dictionary, believe me, in faith-based families, it's a thing!

"Our family dynamic is too good to risk messing it up. Me and the wife are good. We have no pressure. We make good money. The kids are all getting along and killing it at school and supporting each other. Dude, things are too good to mix with the chemistry! Know what I mean?"

No, I don't. Sorry. A little puke comes to my mouth to be honest when I hear this! Who thinks like that anyway? You were expressing the views of a friend, right?

What would you think if I told you that there are foster kids who have never had anyone love them? There are kids who have never seen a loving family, who have no idea what one looks like. What if I told you there were kids who have never ever had a Christmas in a home with a family before? What if I told you that there were kids who have never gone to a family reunion, kids who have never sat down at a table and enjoyed a meal where the family actually talked together? What if I told you there were kids who have never seen the mountains or a beach, kids who have never had a backyard BBQ that didn't end up in a drunken free-for-all?

Would you believe that there are kids who have never had a bedtime story complete with tickles, giggles, and hugs? They're out there, not far away from your house at all. (Pardon me . . . but did you say that you were worried about messing up your home dynamics? Are you kidding me right now?)

At the time of this writing, Dawn and I are shepherding a child who has been in a group home since she was 3 or 4. This past Thanksgiving and Christmas were her first ever in a home with a family. Seeing her fawn over the Christmas decorations going up all over the house was a memory I hope never fades away. At the Christmas dinner table she didn't talk. Not a word. She sat there and watched as our biological family and our other foster daughter laughed, joked, and enjoyed food and family time together.

Ok, fasten your chinstrap and make sure your mouthpiece is in place. The next paragraph might get a bit rough. Are you ready? Here goes. If you skip the next paragraph I pray the fleas of a thousand camels will infest your armpits!

Who said that God wants your family to be a polished trophy that is confined and displayed in the tiny showcase of your local church? Are you kiddin' me? Maybe God wants you to read the Gospel narrative into the life of a young person who has never heard about God's love, God's grace or God's forgiveness.

Ouch. Wow, that was a zinger.

It's a great blessing that your family is legit and "tight," but what about others who weren't fortunate enough to be born into your family? I'm not saying that it is wrong to be wise in the placements you accept, but the bigger question is—what does God want you to do?

What if the good news of the Gospel had stayed in the tiny little upper room with the disciples? Or what if the gospel was only for those privileged enough to be born into full-blooded Jewish families? I for one am glad the blessing of the good news was shared with the Gentiles, and I'd be willing to bet that you are as well. Maybe, just maybe, God gave your family a chemistry, connection, and "mojo" so that your family could be a tool He could use in His greater mission of showing the world His love.

Just a thought.

Lest anyone think my rant to be a bit reckless, let me try to make sure that my position is clear. Should you be careful when you bring children into your home who have been hurt sexually, physically or emotionally? Absolutely. Could they in turn bring that brokenness into play in your family with your children? Of course! Jesus had a wise answer for in situations like this in His words in Matthew 10:16, " . . . Therefore be as wise as serpents and as harmless as doves."

Myth # 3:
I have already raised my family.

"Yeah, Jon, we would be so in, but our kids are grown now and our empty nest isn't exactly attractive for foster kids."

Dude, you are the perfect people for teenagers! Seriously! Wait a minute, don't close the book, hear me out on this one.

For starters, most foster families are afraid of teens. I had been a youth pastor for 16 years and when I found out our first placement was a teen, I thought we were going to be spray-painted orange for Pete's sake! Sure it sounds crazy, but so did committing yourself to 30 years on a mortgage the first time you ever went through closing, right? That's the way it is with fostering teens.

As an empty-nester you can actually focus in on the teenager and truly get involved in their life. You can watch their sport practices, go to their games (and sit far away from them so they aren't too weirded out). Driving them all over creation will prepare you for a retirement career with Uber or Lyft when this is over.

But let's be real. As a veteran parent who has seen a couple of youngsters get through those dreaded teen years, you have been around that block before, and I'm pretty sure you have a t-shirt or two laying around your garage to prove it.

Face it, all teens get crazy weird going through high school—I blame the teachers who gave them so much homework for this! Seriously, you are already experienced, and dare I say qualified, to [illegible] those hormonal years with another teen because you [illegible] of that both you and they will get through this. [illegible] white-haired, sedan-driving, empty-nested friend [illegible] t that many people don't have: a resume that has ex- [illegible] can truly say, "Been there, done that, got the t-shirt." There is a calming force that mature adults bring to a teen that just might be the encouragement they need to age out of foster care and get into a wage-earning career, vocation, or even into a junior college somewhere.

What's the worst that can happen? They cuss you out? What, have you never been F-bombed before? They tell you that they hate you? Like no one has ever told you that before? But what about the gains? The possibilities for gains are infinite!

Myth # 4:
You can't love non-bios as much as bios.

I'm sorry, but THAT IS WRONG ON ABSOLUTELY EVERY LEVEL. (Yes, I was yelling, in a grace-filled sort of way!) For starters, Dawn was not biologically related to me when we met, but I have a serious crush on this woman! We were not biologically related before we were married, that would be weird . . . and illegal in most countries in the world.

I am smitten with our bio family for sure! They are amazing people, even if they are the fruit of my loins (thought I would throw a little King James in there). However, these fosters have come into our hearts. We had one child with us for 14 months that gets

Christmas gifts and birthday presents, and he takes up the lion's share of my wife's iCloud photo stream!

Love is a gift from God, and when God places that solitary one into your family, He gives you the love that child needs!

Myth # 5:
I have heard horror stories about the foster-care system.

And. So. What's your point? If you are asking if the system has problems, the answer is yes. Let me count the ways. It is slow. There are many, many layers of people involved. The levels of care are complicated. The automated phone system is from the pits of Sheol. The time of getting a return phone call from overloaded social workers is slower than a herd of snails traveling through peanut butter. Slower than a one-legged dog on tranquilizers. Slower than molasses in winter. (I actually have a few more, but I'll stop because I can sense that my wife is frowning at me.)

The system is not perfect. Judges aren't perfect. Bio parents aren't perfect. The social workers aren't perfect, and yes, the kids are also not perfect. Not even close. Mental health doctors aren't perfect.

Here's someone else in the system who isn't perfect: YOU! That's right, none of us are perfect either. You will lose your cool, you will lose your head, and you will think at times you are losing your mind.

Are the horror stories about the system true? Probably, yes! Maybe 50% of those horror stories are true.

But do you know what horror story is 100% true? The story that these kids live on a daily basis. What if you could be a part of changing a kid's narrative on life? Every time a child is placed into your home and you give them love, food and a safe environment the KIDS win. That is priceless! Don't let the myths keep you from the joy of changing a life.

Discussion Questions

1. What is your reaction to this statement: "I will get so attached that I won't be able to let go when they leave." Why do people say this?

2. What is your reaction this statement: "It will mess up our family dynamic." What does it show about idols in our life?

3. What is your reaction to this statement: "I have already raised my family." What are some of the advantages that empty-nesters have?

4. What is your reaction to this statement: "You can't love non-bios as much as bios." How does God's gift of love for people instruct us differently?

5. Should the potential horrors of the foster-care system keep us from getting involved in the lives of children?

EPILOGUE

The Proverbs of Fostering

This chapter is devoted to the few . . . the brave . . . the foster-care parents who are in the thick of the battle. Previous chapters were all about recruiting and reasoning with prospective families about why they should get into the game. Finally, this a chapter that is for you, my comrades, my brothers and sisters, my fellow soldiers, my teammates.

Most of what is to follow might sound like a chapter out of the book of Proverbs. I love Proverbs, don't you? Maybe it is my short attention span, or maybe it is the fact that these single stand-alone statements pack a powerful tidbit of wisdom!

Mine are not so deep and not so wide, but they are random encouraging statements that I have gathered and written down over the years from various sources. None are necessarily original with me, although it is true that I have tried to put my own fostering spin on them all.

If you are anything like me, you will have a moment sometime, somewhere when you will doubt your calling, question the mission and plan your resignation from fostering. This chapter is for that moment. Before you actually 14-day that child or send off your resignation email, remember that there is a chapter in this book that has a few words of hope and encouragement for that really bad day.

When You Think About Quitting:

1. When you said yes to bringing that precious soul into your home, you signed up for New Normal 101. New isn't bad (Philippians 3:14). Remember that even the leeks and the garlics look good from the rearview mirror (Numbers 11:5). Embrace the new mission.
2. When you can't see the ending date of the Covid, the silver lining behind the cloud, or the finish line of the placement you have been given, trust God for grace for today (Matthew 6:11).
3. Look how far you have come; remind yourself of all of the things that God has done through your fostering, and encourage yourself that you will reap a full harvest if you don't quit (Galatians 6:9). If you need to quit, go ahead and take the whole day, and we'll see you back at your post tomorrow!
4. Never quit fostering on a bad day or when you feel that you have failed that child. You will second-guess that decision for the rest of your life. If you feel that God wants you to tap out, then do it when you are on top again.
5. Before you 14-day a child, remind yourself of your mission again (Luke 19:10). Jesus lived on-mission, and so do missional foster parents. If it were easy, everyone would be doing it. Remind yourself of the hard places that child has hailed from. A good night sleep just might be all you need to begin tomorrow with a fresh perspective.
6. Enjoy the challenge but remind yourself often that you are not the Hero of the story or the Savior of the world. We are the moons to reflect the Son. We are the John the Baptists to Jesus (John 1:8). He must increase, but we must decrease (John 3:30).
7. You have no idea how close you are to a breakthrough with a child. Tomorrow might be the day when the pendulum swings back the other way. I'm sure Naaman felt like quitting as he was dipping the sixth time in the Jordan (2 Kings 5). Keep on dippin'.

8. Remember that every child is a soul that will live forever somewhere. Look past the bad behaviors and gaze deeply into those precious eyes and listen to their story. That story is very important to God, so it must be important to us. Maybe you have enough gas in the tank to give it another day.
9. At least you haven't quit yet! (Jon Stone 1:1) ROFL!
10. Take time to self-care. Rest. Get away for a break (Mark 6:31). Jesus was known to thrive in the solitary places with His Father; maybe a self-care day will be just what the Doctor ordered for you as well. Taking time off will greatly affect your time-on.

When You Think You Are a Failure:

1. Get in line, take a number and then look at all of the foster parents ahead of you in line who felt like they weren't doing a lick of good either. Failure is par for this course. Lick your wounds, go to Krispy Kreme and get a doughnut. At least you will feel like a happy failure.
2. Crisis will force dependence on God. His strength is made perfect when you feel at your weakest (2 Corinthians 12:9). Weakness is a very good state for missional foster parents to reside in. Your weakness reveals His strength.
3. You saw the cause, you enlisted, you finished the home studies, you opened your home to the fatherless while your peers stood around on the sidelines! You are making things happen, and that's what foster parents do. Tune the radio station of your mind to Spirit radio and get your jam on. Encourage yourself in the Lord like David did when he felt like a failure (1 Samuel 30:6).
4. The game is not over, and some amazing comebacks have happened in the most unlikely scenarios. (Super Bowl LI, Feb. 5, 2017, Falcons were up 28-3 in the third quarter. Final score Patriots 34, Falcons 28). Don't ever count God out of the game. Good Friday was bleak, but Sunday was a whole different story! (Mark 16:9).
5. You are better now than you were before you started this journey. Remember that. You have learned. You have grown. You have been stretched. Your faith is stronger now than it was when you

first began. I could be wrong, but that doesn't sound like failure if you ask me (Romans 8:28).

6. Remind yourself that you have the privilege of being an instrument that God is using (1 Corinthians 1:26).
7. The most valuable commodities in this world are eternal souls, and you are on the front lines of soul rescue (James 1:26-27). Failure might be a premature diagnosis, don't ya think?

When You Wonder If You Are Making a Difference:

1. Jesus is the answer to every crisis, the solution to every problem, and the cure for every pandemic! All you have to do is point people to Him (Philippians 1:26). Even the Sower recorded good results only about 25% of the time (Mark 4:8).
2. Make another emotional love deposit into a child (John 13:34-35). It's like your savings account . . . lots of deposits will allow a few corrective debits! The more you deposit the more you can debit, so love on them again and again.
3. Adapt and overcome (Marine corps purpose statement). After Dr. Seuss wrote his first book, *And to Think I Saw it on Mulberry Street*, it was rejected 28 separate times. But he didn't give up. By the time of his death in 1991, he had sold over 600 million copies of his books in 20 different languages. Remember a just man rises up one more time. (Proverbs 24:16).
4. You, my Good Samaritan teammate, are a part of the healing process (Luke 10:25-37). He is the healer; we are like the Good Samaritan who gets involved, puts them on a horse, cleanses their wounds and sits with them through the night while they are hurting. Healing takes time. Be patient with them like the farmer James referenced in (James 5:7). The only thing that comes up overnight is weeds.
5. Love is the key (1 Corinthians 13:13). Love is an action verb. Love is not a feeling, emotion, idea, notion, song, or emoji. Love is expressive and demanding (Mark 12:31). It requires sacrifice, devotion, and intrusions into your schedules. Love deeply. You are making a difference, trust God to bring fruit in His time.

When You Feel You Are at An Impasse:

1. Pray (James 1:5).
2. Repeat step #1 above.
3. Parent each child differently. "Train up a child" (Proverbs 22:6). Each child is different. Pivot your parenting as needed. Don't underestimate the power of the pivot. Methods will always evolve. Think outside the box. One child needs grace, another needs correction and structure. May God give you wisdom in the moment to know which you should employ.
4. Problem solving is mastering the art of negotiation and compromise. (Win for them + Win for you = Win for the home team; Acts 15:13ff.) James, the pastor of the church in Jerusalem understood negotiations and diffused a volatile, potentially tragic, cultural situation in the early church.
5. Look past the fruit to the root (Matthew 15:18). This is vital for all parenting, not just fostering. The youth in your home who is acting out was probably triggered, so look for the trigger and sidestep the words they used. This is the million-dollar question: "What caused the meltdown?" We may never know what caused the crisis, but if we ask God, He will give us some light into the best next step.
6. Look for other possible solutions. Debrief with God in prayer and dialogue with your mate or with others who have experience in this arena. There is safety in a multitude of counselors (Proverbs 15:22).

A Final Word: Regrets

The other night Dawn and I were walking the sidewalks of our Orcutt subdivision as we often do in the early evenings. The sun was setting over the ridge, the palm trees were bending softly at the urging of the brisk breeze off the ocean, and we were talking through some of the events of the day, which happened to be heavily weighted with updates about our foster kids' lives. The conversation hit a lull and Dawn broke the silence with a question that

I didn't see coming. "Do you have any regrets"? I knew what she meant. She wanted to know if I had any misgivings about our journey in foster care.

It was silent for a while as I thought. After a moment or two I confessed that I did have a regret about our journey into fostering. Her eyes shot over to mine as she reached out and grabbed my hand. I had her full attention because fostering was something that she never pushed on me. "My regret is that I wish that we had entered into fostering sooner! I hate that we waited so long, that I waited so long."

Why should you foster children or get involved in the causes for the fatherless, orphans and wounded children among us? The answer to that question is the thesis of this book—because of the mission! Help children because they are hurting and broken and in need! Foster children because they are being rescued from dark places and they need for someone, anyone to put their arms around them and help them to navigate life.

Maybe God will give you a permanent member of your family through the process! Maybe we have an adoption ahead of us in the years to come! May God's will be done. In the meantime, this book has primarily been a call to stand in the gap and temporarily parent someone's children for them until they can get their act together.

My dear friend, if God has put an interest, a desire, a thought about fostering in your heart, I urge you—follow it. He has put that longing in your heart, and He stands ready to be ALL that you need along the way. He's got you—you can do it with His help. There are some little ones who are going to need you down the road, so let's do this!

Discussion Questions

1. What do you think would discourage foster parents along the way? In your answer, be sure to keep in mind the foster care system, the biological parents, the blending of the foster into the family, the special needs of the child, the additional therapist visits, and the like.

2. In chapter 6 Jon made the statement that he and his wife often feel like failures when it comes to foster youth. What would make a foster parent feel like this?

3. Jon compares foster parents to the Good Samaritan. How does this analogy fit, and how is it different?

4. In the last section above we were reminded to parent each child differently. Should you have different rules for bios than you do for the fosters? What are some rules that might be different and what are some rules that might be the same for all of the children in your home?

5. In the last section Jon encouraged us to "look past the fruit to the root" of the problem. How is this necessary when it comes to foster care? How would this understanding affect the way a parent interacts with their bio child?